Blending
FAMILIES

ALSO BY ELAINE FANTLE SHIMBERG

HOW TO GET OUT OF THE HOSPITAL ALIVE (COAUTHOR)

A HERITAGE OF HELPING: SHRINERS HOSPITALS

LIVING WITH TOURETTE'S SYNDROME

GIFTS OF TIME (COAUTHOR)

DEPRESSION: WHAT FAMILIES SHOULD KNOW

STROKES: WHAT FAMILIES SHOULD KNOW

RELIEF FROM IBS: IRRITABLE BOWEL SYNDROME

TEENAGE PREGNANCY: EXPLAINING THE FACTS

COPING WITH KIDS AND VACATION (COAUTHOR)

TEENAGE DRINKING AND DRIVING: A DEADLY DUO

TWO FOR THE MONEY: A WOMAN'S GUIDE TO A DOUBLE CAREER

MARRIAGE (COAUTHOR)

HOW TO BE A SUCCESSFUL HOUSEWIFE/WRITER

Blending FAMILIES

Elaine Fantle Shimberg

BERKLEY BOOKS, NEW YORK

THE BERKLEY PUBLISHING GROUP
Published by the Penguin Group
Penguin Group (USA) Inc.
375 Hudson Street, New York, New York 10014, USA
Penguin Group (Canada), 90 Eglinton Avenue East, Suite 700, Toronto, Ontario M4P 2Y3, Canada
(a division of Pearson Penguin Canada Inc.)
Penguin Books Ltd., 80 Strand, London WC2R 0RL, England
Penguin Group Ireland, 25 St. Stephen's Green, Dublin 2, Ireland (a division of Penguin Books Ltd.)
Penguin Group (Australia), 250 Camberwell Road, Camberwell, Victoria 3124, Australia
(a division of Pearson Australia Group Pty. Ltd.)
Penguin Books India Pvt. Ltd., 11 Community Centre, Panchsheel Park, New Delhi—110 017, India
Penguin Group (NZ), 67 Apollo Drive, Mairangi Bay, Auckland 1311, New Zealand
(a division of Pearson New Zealand Ltd.)
Penguin Books (South Africa) (Pty.) Ltd., 24 Sturdee Avenue, Rosebank, Johannesburg 2196,
South Africa

Penguin Books Ltd., Registered Offices: 80 Strand, London WC2R 0RL, England

A Berkley Book / published by arrangement with the author

The publisher does not have any control over and does not assume any responsibility for author or third-party
websites or their content.

BLENDING FAMILIES

PRINTING HISTORY
Berkley trade paperback edition / April 1999

ISBN: 978-0-425-16677-2

PRINTED IN THE UNITED STATES OF AMERICA

20   19

TO JOSHUA
Who made me what I am today...
A step-grandmother

ON *P*ARENTING

Your children are not your children.
They are the sons and daughters of Life's longing for itself.
They come through you but not from you,
And though they are with you, yet they belong not to you.
You may give them your love but not your thoughts,
For they have their own thoughts.
You may house their bodies but not their souls,
For their souls dwell in the house of tomorrow,
which you cannot visit, not even in your dreams.
You may strive to be like them, but seek not to
make them like you,
For life goes not backward nor tarries with yesterday.
You are the bows from which your children as
living arrows are sent forth.
The Archer sees the mark upon the path of the
infinite, and He bends you with His might that
His arrows might go swift and far.
Let your bending in the Archer's hand be for gladness;
For even as He loves the arrow that flies,
so He loves also the bow that is stable.

—KAHLIL GIBRAN

ON PARENTING

Your children are not your children.

They are the sons and daughters of Life's longing for itself.

They come through you but not from you,

and though they are with you, yet they belong not to you.

You may give them your love but not your thoughts,

For they have their own thoughts.

You may house their bodies but not their souls,

For their souls dwell in the house of tomorrow,

which you cannot visit, not even in your dreams.

You may strive to be like them, but seek not to
make them like you.

For life goes not backward nor tarries with yesterday.

You are the bows from which your children as
living arrows are sent forth.

The Archer sees the mark upon the path of the
infinite, and He bends you with His might that
His arrows might go swift and far.

Let your bending in the Archer's hand be for gladness;

For even as He loves the arrow that flies,
so He loves also the bow that is stable.

— KAHLIL GIBRAN

Reprinted by permission of Alfred A. Knopf, Inc., from The Prophet, by
Kahlil Gibran, copyright 1923 by Kahlil Gibran and renewed 1951 by
Administration C.T.A. of Kahlil Gibran Estate and Mary G. Gibran.

ACKNOWLEDGMENTS

This book represents the effort and input of many people. I am indebted to all of the men, women, and children who took time to reveal to me their experiences of living in a blended family. They not only were honest in their reactions, but as a group were most anxious for me to encourage others who were about to enter into the world of blended families. "It can work," was their message. Even those with unsuccessful attempts at stepparenting wanted to share what had gone right as well as warn about the pitfalls.

I am particularly appreciative for the help and encouragement I received from Linda Albert, Jackie Favish, Jacquie Kadwit, my niece Karlie Arkin, and my many e-mail friends who I met and grew close to as we "talked" about blended families. Thanks also to the ever-helpful staff at the Tampa-Hillsborough County Public Library.

My very special thanks go to two women in my life. Both were extremely helpful and supportive of this project—my agent, Faith Hamlin, who is always there for me with a laugh and encouragement and my daughter-in-law, Heidi, who like her namesake in

Johanna Spyri's book has brought joy into
our home and gave us Joshua.

I warmly thank my husband of thirty-
seven years, Hinks Shimberg, for his encouragement and love.

CONTENTS

Contents

INTRODUCTION

I grew up in a small town in Iowa. I vividly remember, when I was ten, walking into a five-and-dime store and a clerk saying, "Elaine, your mother's looking for you."

You didn't mess up in Fort Dodge, Iowa. Too many people knew who you were, were looking out for you, and would tell your parents if you didn't behave. That's the meaning of the now well-known African expression, "It takes a village to raise a child."

Today, with one of every two marriages ending in divorce, various combinations of a child's parents, stepparents, and extended family often are inhabitants of that village. Children must learn to adjust to a staggering array of newly formed kinships, relationships that bring with them both emotional baggage and numerous issues that need to be resolved. Among them are:

- Who's got the power?

- What rights do stepparents have?

- How should school issues be determined when there's joint custody?

- How can schools work with divorced parents and the stepparents to reduce unnecessary stress and conflict?

- How should money management issues be resolved?

- How can the pediatrician and his/her office balance the demands of the divorced parents and become sympathetic to the needs of the stepparents?

. How can conflicts be resolved and compromises be negotiated between such issues as prep school or public school and summer plans, weighing camp where dad's family attended for generations against the seashore with mom's parents?

. What is the role of step-grandparents with their step-grandchildren? What rights do they have?

. Who gets tickets for the college student's graduation when only two are issued for the traditional "mom" and "dad?"

. Does the stepparent have the right to discipline a child? If so, how and when?

. How does a "significant other" handle the child when he/she is living under the same roof?

. Whose rules from which household prevail concerning television viewing, dating, and other issues?

. How should you handle emotions—the children's and your own?

. Who gets the child for Christmas? Passover? Birthdays?

. Which father walks the daughter down the aisle at her wedding?

. How many sets of parents fit under the wedding canopy at a Jewish wedding?

The answers to these questions probably were never taught at our mother's knee. It's unlikely that they were taught in any classroom either. For many of us growing up, the only stepparents we knew were (1) those who had married a playmate's widowed mother or widower father and (2) Cinderella's stepmother and the stepparents from other fairy tales. We had not, as yet, met Carol and Mike Brady.

It's doubtful that many of us thought as children, "When I grow up, I want to be a stepparent." And yet, today more Americans are part of a second marriage family than a first. One out of five children under the age of eighteen is a stepchild. Although it's difficult to get firm statistics because of the many permeations of stepfamilies, it's estimated that there are 5.2 million stepfamilies in the United States alone, with more than 1,300 new ones formed *each* day.

Most of these families are merely getting by, coping one day at a time on a catch-as-catch-can basis, as they balance precariously on guidelines that worked for the nuclear families of the 1950s but offer few footholds for today's blended families. Institutions, such as schools, churches and synagogues, hospitals, scouting and summer camps, change at a snail's pace, using regulations and procedure books that are sadly out-of-date. "Family values," the mantra replacing "God, country, and mother" on the lips of TV producers, politicians, and pulpit people is meaningful, but neglects to define "family" in today's practical and realistic terms.

Just which family's values are we to emulate? Stepdad's? Mom's? Dad's? Stepmom's? Stepdad's parents? Stepmom's parents? How many grandparents can dance on the head of a pin, today's philosophers might ask? Whose values are "right" or "best?" For many blended families, the few rules that do exist change so rapidly, they might as well be written on an Etch-a-Sketch pad.

New support systems and foundations need to be devised to keep all involved—children, parents, stepparents, grandparents, extended families, teachers, coaches, and others—on a functioning and an even keel. But one of the problems is that there is no "one way fits all" for stepfamilies. Each is unique, with its own composition, personalities, and problems. Over one hundred years ago, Tolstoy wrote in his great novel *Anna Karenina*, "All happy families resemble one another; every unhappy family is unhappy in its own way." But happy blended families seldom resemble one another; and every blended family must cope in its own way.

So, if each stepfamily is unique, how can there be a guidebook for them? Where is the list of "ten things to do in order to have a successful blended family?" Actually, you'll find many different lists here (along with other hints), but consider *Blending Families* to be a work in progress, a smorgasbord of suggestions, of tips for you to use to see if they fit your particular stepfamily and its needs.

Although the experts—sociologists, family therapists, members of the clergy, psychologists, and psychiatrists—have compiled statistics and studied the problems inherent in blended families, *Blending Families* does not focus on merely the problems. Instead, it offers solutions, ideas that have been implemented and found to be successful by those who have actually used them—individuals who are part of a stepfamily. After all, who better to advise their peers than those who are in the trenches, who have walked in these paths before them and have learned to avoid the pitfalls? While including data from experts in the field, *Blending Families* is foremost a practical "this-is-how-it-worked-for-me" book, focusing on the strengths of successful stepfamilies.

The majority of the material for this book is based on interviews with those involved in stepfamilies, including biological parents, stepparents, stepchildren, adult stepchildren, grandparents, step-grandparents, and extended family members both from the original family and the stepfamily. In addition to one-on-one in-person interviews, I used questionnaires, e-mail interviews, and various stepparenting bulletin boards on the Internet. Word-of-mouth concerning what I was writing triggered numerous long-distance calls from Maine to California from people urging me to include suggestions on what worked for them. Many of them also offered to map out where the stepparenting potholes were located, so others following behind them might avoid mishaps.

I was particularly interested in the reactions and suggestions by the "double-steppers," adult children who were stepchildren, who are also now stepparents. In all, I gathered personalized information from 106 individuals, as well as using available literature and research studies.

This approach not only ensures that the real and most vital issues concerning stepfamilies will be covered, but also that some unique and creative approaches devised by those most intimately involved can be learned and adapted to your own needs.

Blending Families is an easy-to-read, problem-solving guide, helping parents and stepparents alike to discover solutions to issues not faced by previous generations of parents, especially in the areas of discipline, money management, and communication, especially with a former spouse. Often, the estranged biological parents are so engaged in a power struggle with each other that they inadvertently have turned the power over to the kids. A separate chapter on dealing with stress addresses one of the major problems both parents and their stepparenting spouses must learn to handle.

There's no doubt that stepfamilies are different from original families. But it is not an issue of "abnormal" versus "normal" or "bad" versus "good." Many stepfamilies are happy, well-functioning, and nurturing relationships, but just as with original family groupings, this just doesn't happen; it takes effort, energy, and enthusiasm, along with communication, compromise, and caring. It can be done; it is being done. You'll learn how by the real life stories of the people you are about to meet.

CHAPTER ONE

For Whom the Wedding Bells Toll

"All weddings, except those with shotguns in evidence, are wonderful."

—LIZ SMITH,
columnist, *New York Daily News*

Your wedding day! The words conjure up visions of a bride in traditional white gown and veil, a nervous groom bolstered by his best man, and a manic mother-of-the-bride alternating copious tears with organizational know-how, efficiency, and effectiveness that would have put General Norman Schwarzkopf to shame. A Norman Rockwell picture.

Your second wedding day, especially if you are entering into not only a state of holy matrimony, but also into the state commonly referred to as stepparenting, bi-nuclear families, or blended families, is far different. The maid-of-honor may drag her American Girl doll behind her; the best man may have his Little League jersey under his tuxedo shirt. Although the honor attendants may view the ceremony itself as either exciting or boring, there's no doubt that the vows being taken by the bride and groom also affect the accompanying offspring in a very personal sense. The tears you may see running down the cheeks of your children during the marriage service probably are not tears of joy for your happiness.

In a very real sense, children often can be riding shotgun at their parent's wedding, not forcing it to take place, but rather wanting to empty a few well-placed shells at the wedding bells. Although the kids may "hold their peace" during the service itself, they may be harboring feelings why this man and this woman should not be united in holy matrimony.

▪ BECOMING A STEPCHILD MEANS HAVING ▪
TO SAY GOOD-BYE TO A DREAM

Most experts agree that children of a divorce usually hang on to the fantasy that one day their parents will be reunited and things will return to the way it used to be (minus the fighting). After all, didn't Elizabeth Taylor once remarry Richard Burton? But when the parent has agreed to marry another person, that hope is shattered. The wedding bells toll a finality to the children, ringing in the realization that a new relationship is being formed, one that affects the youngsters on a great many levels.

Long before you pick out the rings, buy the wedding dress, or plan a honeymoon for three or four or more, make time to discuss many of the vital issues that will affect your children (and could affect your marriage) long after the remarriage has taken place. Although your children may not be able to verbalize what they're thinking, chances are good that all but the very littlest ones have fears about "what happens when . . ." Remember, kids, like most of us, are primarily concerned about what happens to them.

"WHERE WILL WE LIVE?"

Whenever possible, it's always best to pick a neutral territory, a house, condo, or apartment that neither parent nor stepparent has lived in before. Otherwise, the stepparent may feel as though it really isn't his or her house. Redecorating, which seems to be a fairly benign procedure, can become fraught with no-win problems when it is seen as someone else's house.

A woman who married a widower with a fourteen-year-old daughter gave up trying to make the old homestead reflect her tastes. "My step-daughter threw a tantrum when I moved so much as a chair from the spot her mother had placed it in. Forget my thoughts of getting rid of the heavy velvet drapes and putting in something light and airy. I felt like I was in prison and the ghost of my husband's first wife was my warden."

In another blended family, however, the stepmother asked for her teenage stepdaughter's thoughts in redecorating the room. Although the youngster hesitated at first, not wanting to be disloyal to her mother's memory, she got caught up in the excitement of selecting fabrics and paint swatches and the two became close working on the project. Just a reflection of the different personalities of the youngsters? Perhaps. But it also shows you probably get more flies with honey than vinegar, just as Mother said.

"WHICH ROOM DO I GET?"

Possessions take on emotional content when a blended family is trying to work out who gets what room. A child who may have been the eldest with the choice room before his or her parent remarried may suddenly become the baby or the middle child. Losing the "best" room to a new stepsibling can create tremendous jealousies and unnecessary rivalries. Two same-sex stepsiblings, each of whom had his or her own bedroom before the remarriage, may discover that they have to share a room in this blended family. While they may eventually become buddies, especially if they are about the same age, there will probably be an extended period of marking one's turf before the dust settles. Housing issues for blended families becomes a juggling act far more complex than ones faced by university housing personnel. Those assignees know they are only stuck in a particular room for a semester or at worst, a year.

• BECOMING A STEPPARENT CREATES • A KALEIDOSCOPE OF CHANGES

Clark Kent's hasty transformation in the telephone booth, allowing him to emerge as Superman, is nothing compared to the myriad changes confronting the man or woman becoming a stepparent. Both, however, require super strength, not to mention patience and a sense of humor.

Regardless of the circumstances—both individuals in the couple having children from a former marriage, only one person having children, or becoming single through divorce or death, but having children—remarriage with children poses many similar problems that must be acknowledged early and faced as a united family.

Begin to discuss these issues *before* the wedding takes place. Let the kids meet each other as soon as you know that you will be marrying. The kids don't have to like each other, but they should be expected to treat their future stepsiblings with respect. Couples who plan for the pre-wedding blending of the two families can set up rules for behavior that should carry into the blended family in the days that follow.

THERE ARE POTENTIAL CRITICS IN THE WINGS

In a second marriage that creates a blended family, the off-stage cast of characters usually outnumbers the members of the wedding party. There may be family and friends, many of whom are shaking their heads and wondering why you are taking on the task of raising someone else's child. Your intended's ex-spouse may worry that you're going to interfere with discipline or change child support and/or custody arrangements. The children are uneasy about this "stranger" (who they may have enjoyed being with during the dating phase) moving into their home and changing the ways things were.

THE CHALLENGE TO MAKE THINGS "PERFECT" THIS TIME

The majority of us who step up to the altar a second time mutter the mantra, "It's got to be better the second time around." If the first marriage ended in divorce, there is some sense of failure, regardless whose "fault" we know it was. If it ended with the spouse's death, there are feelings of regret and guilt still lingering like June bugs around the porch light. We set before us an impossible task: to be perfect this time.

THE DESIRE TO "LOVE THESE CHILDREN LIKE THEY'RE MY OWN"

Regardless how much someone adores children and loves their parent, it's difficult to love someone else's children as much as you do your own. Those parents who have their own children may try to love their stepchildren just the same, but those who were candid with me during interviews admitted that it was a "different kind of love."

In answer to my question, "What do you wish you knew before you became a stepparent?" the overwhelming response was, "That it was okay not to love my stepchildren right away. I felt so guilty, thinking it was just something wrong with me."

"GETTING TO KNOW YOU" TAKES A WHILE

We live in an age of immediacy, where letters are e-mailed, memos are faxed, and you can buy a complete dinner fully cooked and ready-to-eat to take home and zap in the microwave. No wonder stepparents and biological parents think things will go great because the couple loves one another and "the kids seem to get along."

But families aren't created in an instant. You can't add water and mix until happiness and a strong relationship thickens. It takes time for a stepparent to learn the family's codes—their inside jokes and references. It takes time for kids to trust an outsider who claims he or she doesn't want to replace their "real" mom or dad. It takes time for a family to work out the lumps, to blend. According to many experts, including Drs. John and Emily Visher, founders of the Stepfamily Association of America, it takes about a year and a half.

"If I could go back in time and do it all over again," said a step-mother of more than a dozen years, "I'd start by reading everything I possibly could about stepfamilies with the idea that all of it could and probably would happen in mine. I'd have a lot of long family talks about expectations and boundaries and probably even involve a counselor who specializes in stepfamily issues to prevent the big issues from causing major problems."

So when is the honeymoon over? Many say it doesn't even start when you remarry with children on the scene. You hit the ground running. That's why it's important to make the time—note, I didn't say *have* the time, but rather to make it—to be alone together as husband and wife, to help your marriage relationship grow and develop. Privacy is something precious that has to be carefully protected, like a fragile flower. The kids may not like it when you go away for the weekend or spend an hour after dinner together in "grown up" time. But it's important for them in the long run. See Chapter Five for more suggestions on Adult Time.

"We took our kids on the honeymoon with us," said stepparents of two different families. "I thought it would help the family bond sooner," said one. "What it did was to create a lot of tension from the beginning. If my wife and I had it to do over, we'd take a week by ourselves to catch our breath before reentry." The second family concurred.

The burden for the success of a blended family must rest on the husband and wife. As parents, you both must dedicate yourselves to making this marriage work by:

· perfecting your communication skills
· developing patience

· using your sense of humor
· pledging commitment to one another and to the marriage

Then, as a team working together for the good of your family, you should be able to overcome the difficulties that are inherent in merging two families, blending while still allowing for individual differences and respecting the children's other family. It can be done. It is being done. But the couples that are doing it best seem to be the ones that begin with strengthening their marriage first. If your marriage is strong, the children will have your firm bond to lean against when they most need support.

CHAPTER TWO

Telling the Players

"A name is a kind of face whereby one is known."

—THOMAS FULLER
17th-century English clergyman

Although William Shakespeare wrote in *Romeo and Juliet*, "What's in a name? That which we call a rose by any other name would smell as sweet," those in blended families know that isn't exactly so. What we call a person is packed with a great deal of emotion and symbolism.

In many cultures, children have one name at birth and are given a symbolic name at adolescence or adulthood, or after performing a specific feat. Writers often take a pseudonym or pen name to disguise their gender or to protect their identity. Actors also have been known to exchange their names for one more easily pronounced by their fans or just to create a different image. Contrary to what Shakespeare wrote, names do color perceptions, and that's why they take on such an importance in blended families.

Our English language, as rich as it is, has yet to coin a word that properly defines "stepfamily." It's not that psychologists and sociologists haven't tried. But "stepfamily" itself is a word that is still synonymous to many with "broken home." If you have to use the word "stepfamily," I prefer to think of it as "stepping up to reorganize a family grouping."

Although some experts prefer the term, "reconstituted family," I really don't. To me, "reconstituted family" sounds as though all you have to do is to add a little water and you can make the family just as it was before.

But it won't be. You'll always have some "left over" parts, like an ex-spouse, ex-grandparents, former aunts and uncles, and all those cousins, second cousins, and cousins once-removed. They can't be stuck in a drawer, forgotten like the extra wing nuts from the kids' swing set. Usually, the ex-relatives remain a part of the child's world. Your former parents-in-law still remain your child's grandparents. *You* may have divorced their kin, but your child hasn't. Besides, most children need as much love and attention as possible.

By the same token, "remarried family" also doesn't work for me. Families don't get remarried, only the bride and groom do. Although the marriage ceremony obviously affects many others and establishes new relationships, the family isn't married (and the family can't get divorced if things don't work out).

I prefer the term, "blended family," because it suggests mixing of different ingredients (in this case, people), and also reminds us that we have to keep working to combine the various components in order to smooth out the lumps. Perhaps the term should actually be "blending family" because it's an on-going process, ever-changing and always fluid.

▪ UNDERSTANDING THE IMPORTANCE OF NAMES ▪

In 1897, Edmond Rostand wrote *Cyrano de Bergerac*, a well-known play (also made into a movie later with Jose Ferrer) about a French author and soldier who had a very long nose. In one scene, Cyrano recites a list of synonyms that could have been used rather than calling his proboscis long. The point was, that regardless what his rather long nose was called, it was still perceived by everyone as just that, a rather long nose.

Anyone who has been burdened with a funny sounding name, initials that spell out silly words, or had an unpleasant nickname knows how emotionally packed a name can be. Compare the self-image of a youngster who is dubbed "Piggy" to the one called "Tiger." Or the burden of a boy with the initials "T.O.Y" or "S.I.S."

Naming anything is usually a complex and stressful process. Most of us are very aware of the power of names to conjure up images of strength, respect, and acceptance. Name books, complete with the meanings and derivatives of each name, line the shelves of book stores and libraries to help the proud parents of a baby or even the owners of a new puppy or kitten come up with a name that perfectly suits the particular individual. Owners of new sports franchises or businesses often turn to advertising agencies, spending thousands of dollars in the process, to create "the perfect name." Yet, to my knowledge, no book has yet been published to help stepchildren deal with the name crisis: "What do I call my father's new wife or my mother's new husband?" or to advise stepparents how they should refer to their stepkids.

Stepchildren often struggle with the need to call the new parent something without feeling disloyal to their biological same-sex parent. Some of them resolve the problem by calling the newcomer nothing. Yet this absence of any name speaks highly of the status of the relationship at that time. Fortunately, over time, many no-names have received fond nicknames, dubbed by those same kids who were troubled in the beginning of the association.

▪ TAKING THE LEAD ▪

Rather than remaining a "no-name," take the lead as the adult in the relationship and offer some suggestions as soon as you plan to marry. Most experts agree that you shouldn't demand to be called "Mom" or "Dad," even if you have an overwhelming desire to be called that. If the child's same sex parent is still alive, there will be resentment (from the child and that parent) who feel as though you are trying to be seen as a replacement. If the parent is dead, there will be even a stronger feeling that you are putting yourself in that parent's place. While time may let the youngster's guard down so he or she feels comfortable calling you "Mom" or "Dad," it should come from the child, not from you.

Offer some suggestions. "You should call me whatever makes you feel comfortable," is a good beginning. "You may call me by my first name or whatever you like," is another opening, although you may be shocked by (and stuck with) the resulting appellation.

Remember that although the name is important in what it symbolizes, the most vital issue is the relationship you and your stepchild are creating. Don't become so focused on the name discussion that you injure your budding relationship. People, kids and adults alike, often change what they call someone. It isn't written in stone.

Early in my marriage, I called my mother-in-law "Mother S." It made her sound like a Mother Superior in a convent. Later, as our relationship drew closer, I felt moved to change my name for her to "Mama." It was done without conversation, as I remember, and neither of us ever referred to the name change. I'm sure, however, that she was aware it marked a deepening fondness and love on my part.

As your relationship with your stepchildren becomes closer and the youngsters feel more comfortable with you, they may one day, rather nonchalantly suddenly surprise you with a new name. Let the intimacy grow naturally, rather than trying to force it.

> "I would love my stepson to call me 'Dad,'" said a stepfather of a five-year-old who calls him by his first name. "But I know that's not realistic. He'd feel disloyal to his biological father by doing so. I always feel awkward when someone says, 'This must be your son,' and I have to answer, 'Actually, he's my stepson.' I wish there were another way of expressing our relationship, like 'I'm his second dad.'"

• CREATING NICKNAMES CAN DENOTE •
SPECIAL AFFECTION

If we give them enough time, kids often devise their own name for a stepparent. While it may take them a while to work through the emotional issues for stepparents, they seem to have no difficulty in naming their grandparents or stepgrandparents. Most of us know how creative youngsters can be in this task. My sister and I called my maternal grandmother "Mamoo" because as a toddler my older sister had heard our mother call her "Mother," and she couldn't pronounce it properly.

My stepgrandson calls me "Grammy," his maternal grandmother "Grams," and his stepmother's mother "Noni." His now deceased paternal grandmother was called "Ga Ga." Confusing for us, perhaps, but he had no difficulty even at four knowing who was who.

A stepmother reported that her stepchildren had been somewhat cool to her since the marriage and had referred to her as "Her," until one night they watched *Gone with the Wind* on television together. She cried so hard during the movie that the kids were touched. They started calling her "Gonda" (for "Gone with the Wind") and it stuck. From that time on, their relationship improved.

Some younger children will call their stepparent by an adaptation of "mother" or "dad," which could be "Mama," "Mom Mary," or "Mommy M," or "Papa John," "Daddy J," "Papa," and so on. Others just continue to call their stepparents by their first name, which is what they used when their biological parent was in the dating relationship.

▪ REMEMBER THE RULE OF THREE ▪

Although you may have your own needs in what you would like to be called, you probably are going to have to accept what the kids come up with. If it isn't what you would have preferred, be patient. They may change it once or twice more. (See Chapter Fifteen for more on the naming issue.)

Remember the Rule of Three when you are struggling with "The Name Game."

1. *What are my needs?*
Your need may be to be accepted (or perceived by others to be accepted) by your stepchildren and, to this end, you may prefer to be called "Mom" or "Dad."

2. *What are the children's needs?*
The kids need to feel loyal to their biological parent. For them to call you "Mom" or "Dad," means in their eyes that they are re-

placing that parent, even if the parent has died. Therefore, it makes them uncomfortable to use those emotionally laden terms.

3. *How can a compromise be achieved?*

Communicate to the youngsters that although you would love for them to call you "Mom" or "Dad," you will understand if this makes them uncomfortable. Give them permission to consider their options. With the emotional pressure removed, they may come up with a special name that you like (almost as much) and that shows their caring, appreciation, and respect for your consideration and sensitivity.

As for your concern regarding what others may think if your stepchildren call you by your first name, rather than "Mother" or "Dad," my advice is to let it go. You're supposed to be the mature adult in this scenario. Stop living your life in the shadow of what others may think. You can only control what you think and isn't that more important?

CHAPTER THREE

Communication

"The deepest hunger of the human heart is to be understood."[1]

STEPHEN R. COVEY

*P*robably one of the most important skills to develop when you're part of a blended family is effective communication. Vital in all personal interactions, it's especially needed in blended families because of the number of people involved. It is no longer just Mom and Dad and the kids; there also are former spouses and their mates, stepparents, stepsiblings, half-siblings, and a ballooned extended family. If you have ever played the childhood game of "Telephone," you know how messed up a simple message can get after it goes through a number of repetitions.

It's also important to work on your communication skills, because in a blended family you're mixing apples and oranges—two different families—and trying to make a fruit salad. Even when you succeed (and most attempts eventually do), you may have created the desired fruit salad, but it's still made up of different ingredients. That's because each family comes to a remarriage with a different set of communication styles that may or may not be compatible with each other. What the members of one family actually say and how they say it may be totally misunderstood by members of the other family.

Understand this phenomenon and be patient. It takes a while to learn any new language. While you may have been talking since you were about fourteen months of age, the making of words has little to do with communication, any more than the ability to stand erect makes you a candidate for the Iron Man competition. It's a beginning, nothing more.

---

[1]Stephen R. Covey, *The Seven Habits of Highly Effective Families*, (New York, 1997), 213, Golden Books.

▪ LEARNING THE DIALECT ▪

Just as each area of every country has its own unique dialect that can be immediately identified by linguistic experts, families also tend to develop their special style of communication that often seems to be a complex code to outsiders. Some families use sarcasm to express themselves, even when speaking fondly to one another. Others may do a lot of yelling or use understatement. Some families discuss everything and everybody openly, while others are more introspective and never discuss problem issues or they may have certain areas (such as finances, sex, death, or illness) that are totally off-limits for discussion. Expressing any type of emotional feeling is taboo in some families, whereas in others, talk of fears, anger, and sadness is not only accepted, but is actually encouraged. No wonder then that when two families are blending or even consider themselves to be blended, these differences can create confusion and tension.

In addition, words and body language may also have different meanings from family to family and also vary from culture to culture. A teenager may shrug and say, "Whatever," when asked for an opinion. His or her biological family know this means the adolescent has no viewpoint one way or another, is laid-back, and is willing to do whatever the majority decides. A new stepparent, however, may take offense, interpreting this behavior as the teenager's being rude.

A youngster brought up in a household where handshakes between father and son were the norm and kisses were few may withdraw in embarrassment or discomfort from a spontaneous affectionate hug or pat on the shoulder from a new stepparent. A teenager, used to a household that holds its emotions in tight check, may feel awkward when a stepparent talks openly about personal feelings on a sensitive issue. As a newcomer to the family, the stepparent often is as totally lost as if he or she had suddenly been transported to a foreign land without any knowledge of the language or cultural differences.

What can you do about it? Don't wait until you feel frustrated, confused, rejected, or irritated. Give immediate feedback. Ask for clarification by saying, "Do you mean . . . ?" Or "I think I hear you saying . . ." If you have misunderstood, ask for a translation. Ask your stepchild directly if your natural show of affection makes him or her feel uncomfortable. Respect the response, even if you know you will eventually bring the kid around. Don't worry, you'll pick up the family's dialect before you know it.

■ MIND-READING IS NOT A FORM OF COMMUNICATION ■

It's easy to assume that your spouse, kids, and stepchildren should "know" what you're trying to say. When they don't understand you, you get frustrated. "If he loved me, he'd know how I felt," one woman complained about her new husband. Then she admitted that one of the causes for the demise of her first marriage was probably poor communication skills.

Don't expect your loved ones to guess what's on your mind—or try to guess what's on theirs. For most of us, mind reading is not an exact science, nor a parlor trick that we have mastered. We tend to create our own interpretations, based on our own past history and the emotion of the moment.

If you're confused about the meaning of something you're hearing from your spouse, stepchildren, or your own kids, request more information or try to paraphrase and ask, "Is this what you mean?" Don't be surprised if you get an odd look in return. You may be way off base. If so, aren't you glad you asked?

When you're talking to your family and sense that you aren't getting the response you anticipated, ask them to restate what they think you've said. Many family feuds and hurt feelings originate in miscommunication, based in the thought that family members should be able to read each other's minds. They can't.

■ LISTENING IS A VITAL PART OF COMMUNICATION ■

There is much more to communication than what you say and how you say it. A vital part of effective communication involves good listening skills, which most of us woefully lack. Think about the last time you drove into a gas station for directions. The attendant verbally gave you the information, accompanied by a great deal of hand waving. You nodded, climbed back into the car, and then realized you had no idea what you had just been told. Why? You hadn't listened.

Industry knows that a great deal of time and money is lost because of poor listening skills. That's why many top businesses bring experts into their companies to conduct seminars that teach their employees how to listen. It's also the reason that over forty-eight percent of colleges and universities now offer listening instruction to their students.

"I am convinced," says Rabbi Richard Birnholz of Congregation Schaarai Zedek in Tampa, Florida, "that most miscommunication occurs because instead of listening, instead of really listening, we are too busy holding our hearings. And there is a difference between listening and holding a hearing. When we listen, we put the other person first. We respond to *their* needs and react sensitively to their feelings. When we hold hearings, we put ourselves first and listen judgmentally. We begin with our own agenda and then, without listening to the other person at all, make our point or make the other person's word fit our expectations."

So put down the television channel clicker and listen to what your family members are trying to say to you. No, don't just hold it in your hand. Put the darn thing down and listen. Focus on the speaker, not on the television screen.

ACTIVE LISTENING

Just as the tree falling in the forest miles from civilization is said to make no sound because no one hears it, effective communication can not take place unless someone hears it. That's why you need to let your stepchild know you are listening when he or she talks to you. It not only is a compliment, it also opens the way for further conversation and a closer relationship. How can you show that you are "all ears?"

1. Put down whatever is in your hands, such as the newspaper, a pen, or knitting.

2. Sit down so you're looking eye-to-eye with the kids, not towering over them.

3. Maintain eye contact, unless you sense that makes the youngster uncomfortable.

4. Give verbal cues, such as "I see," "Oh," or "Uh huh."

5. Focus on what's being said, not what you're going to answer.

6. Don't interrupt.

7. If the subject's somewhat controversial, keep your mind open while holding your emotions in check.

8. Don't jump to conclusions.

9. Don't look at your watch or show impatience. If it isn't a good time to talk, admit it and reschedule for the earliest available time.

10. Don't invade the child's space.

11. Don't feel you have to fill a silence; often a pause prepares the way for more honest communication.

12. Let the answering machine pick up if the phone rings. You may lose the moment with your stepchild if you interrupt the conversation to answer the telephone.

LISTENING DOESN'T MEAN AGREEMENT

You can be a good listener without being judgmental or feeling a need to give your own opinion. Listening does not mean you agree with what's being said. If one of your stepchildren is complaining about a classmate, it's better to merely confirm what you're hearing by saying, "It sounds as though Katherine made you very angry," rather than announcing, "I really don't like that girl. I think that Katherine character's nothing but trouble." For all you know, your stepchild and Katherine will make up and be close friends by the end of the next day, and you'll have to eat those words and spend the next few years wondering if Katherine knows what you said about her.

SET THE SCENE FOR LISTENING

Try to make time that is good for you to be involved one-on-one with each of your stepchildren. They may not have anything to say or will answer, "Fine," when you ask how school was. But if you're there and you demonstrate an interest, eventually they'll open up. Ask more open-ended questions that beg more than a "yes" or "no" answer, such as "What was on the math test?" rather than "Was the math test hard?"

Plan ahead to prevent being interrupted by turning on the telephone answering machine, turning off the television, or by giving toddlers something to play with so you can talk with the older child. Little ones often tend to be jealous when the grown-ups show attention to others and will seem to come swarming out of the woodwork just when your stepchild begins to open up for the first time.

▪ BE AWARE OF BODY LANGUAGE ▪

There is a vast array of nonverbal messages we send both when speaking and listening, some of which may be the antithesis of what our words are saying. We may say we have time to listen, but our body language can give us away. Experts say that more than half of what we communicate is expressed not in words, but in body language. These saboteurs include our facial expressions, such as smiling or frowning, eye contact (or lack of it), and body movements such as changes in posture and hand gestures. According to Florence Wolff, professor emeritus of the University of Dayton and an expert on listening skills, "there are two hundred thirty-five different facial expressions."

Beware of sending these double messages, such as saying, "I'm interested," while glancing at papers on the desk or letting your eyes glance around the room. If you can't give your full attention to the speaker, whether it is your spouse, children, or stepchildren, say honestly, "I'm really tied up now. Could I get back to you in five minutes?" And then be sure you do so.

You need to look at whoever is speaking to you as well. "Eighty percent of the speaker's message comes from nonverbal cues," says Dr. Wolff. "If the listener isn't looking, he or she is going to miss eighty percent of the meaning."

All nonverbal messages aren't bad, of course. When you pat your stepson on the back and say, "Good job," or smile and give a big wink, you're accenting the truth of your words. A hug says a lot when your stepdaughter doesn't make the team or you just think she looks great. Go slow at first, however. Be sure the kids are receptive to hugs and pats. If they're not, they may slowly learn to be. Just don't overwhelm them at first. Take your cues from them, especially if they are teenagers.

TOUCHING IS A FORM OF COMMUNICATION

You may come from a touchy-feely family where hugs, kisses, and stroking were commonplace. In these physical close families, nonverbal communication often is expressed through a pat on the hand, cuddling, putting your arm around a loved one's shoulder, playful wrestling, or responding to a family member's request that, "I need some hugging time."

Your stepfamily, however, may be one where casual physical contact is seldom experienced. The family members don't flop on the floor together or squeeze in to make room for one more on the couch. Affectionate pats and kisses hello and good-bye are rare. Your playful request for a "family sandwich" or a group hug, may cause your stepkids to look at you as though you just flew in from another planet. Be aware of these differences in communication techniques, some of which may be cultural in nature, and be sensitive to them. While you eventually may be able to change some of these communication behaviors, it won't happen overnight. If you move too quickly, your stepchildren may feel threatened and pull away.

Sometimes kids become more receptive to touching as a form of comfort and caring when there is an "our child," born into the family. Hugging, patting, and caressing infants is a natural reaction for most people. Even teenagers who pull away when you try to hug them will usually want to reach out to hug or kiss an infant. Slowly the youngsters may realize that what's good for the "bonus baby" is also good for them.

ALL KIDS ARE CLOSED-MOUTHED AT TIMES

If, despite your best efforts, you can't get your stepchildren to open up, don't despair. *All* kids (especially adolescents and teenagers) have moments when they don't feel talkative at all, especially to any type of an adult, and most especially to any type of a parent. It doesn't matter if they come from loving, close families with biological parents who are madly devoted to each other or if they are your stepchildren who are just getting to know you. You may hear these same kids talking on the telephone for hours to their friends, but when you offer to listen, they have nothing to say.

Stop beating yourself up, guiltily thinking that it's your fault. It isn't. It's merely their way of protecting their privacy and is part of growing up. It's also just one of the more frustrating aspects of having adolescents and teenagers. Fortunately, just when you figure they've secretly joined a monastery and have taken a vow of silence, the kids you remember from the days you were dating their parent (i.e., before you became a stepparent), reappear and demonstrate that they knew how to talk all along.

Take heart from a study published in the September 10, 1997 *Journal of the American Medical Association*. It concludes that "feeling loved, understood, and paid attention to by parents helps teenagers avoid high-risk activities . . ." By working toward developing strong communication skills with all members of your blended family, you'll be strengthening that sense of "feeling loved, understood, and paid attention to."

▪ MAKING TIME TO TALK ▪

We all have the same amount of time each day, yet in blended families there may be many additional demands on this time. With joint custody, you may only have the children for a few days each week or every other week. You also may have additional children from another marriage coming to live with you for part of the time. It makes scheduling one-on-one time more difficult, not to mention finding a place that's conducive to private conversations. Yet by being creative, you can and should set this time aside.

ENCOURAGE YOUR STEPCHILDREN TO JOIN YOU FOR ONE-ON-ONE ACTIVITIES

Martha, a stepmother to an eleven-year-old girl, created a special break time around 4:00 p.m. so the two of them could sit down to have cookies and conversation. Fortunately, Martha was a freelance illustrator who worked out of the home and could easily schedule this time out from her work. "It began informally," she said, "and irregularly, as my stepdaughter originally told me she thought it was a dumb idea and that she didn't even like the cookies I bought. But when we started baking her favorite cookies together and put them on my good Wedgewood blue china, she came around. Now she's confided that her friends think our "C&C" time is really 'cool.' And we've started doing more cooking together, something I'm good at that she enjoys."

More active one-on-one activities work equally well. Walking together is a good time to share confidences and work out problems, especially for youngsters who feel a little uncomfortable opening up to a stepparent at first. So is washing the car together, running errands in the car (providing you turn off the radio so you can hold a real conversation), going to a ball game, fixing a gourmet or ethnic dinner, working in the family flower or vegetable garden, or even folding and ironing clothes. In the days before the modern electric dishwasher, I remember having "quality time" with my own mother as we washed and dried the dishes.

USE HUMOR TO INTRODUCE COMMUNICATION

Humor is often a subtle way to stimulate conversation with your stepchildren, as long as you are careful never to use it at their expense. Many youngsters—even teenagers—respond to puns and knock-knock jokes with a groan, but then hasten to supply one of their own favorites.

Young children share a sense of the ridiculous. One day my daughter-in-law asked me to take Joshua, her four-year-old, to play-school for her as she had an early morning meeting. It was a change from his daily routine and I was a little worried that he might be upset or fussy. The two of us sang silly songs on the way from the house to school. (That's one of the nice things about little ones: they never complain about your being off-key.) Before getting him out of the backseat of the car, I said seriously, "Well, let's see. I've got the lunch box, the permission slip, the baseball cap . . . hum . . . am I forgetting something? What could it be?"

He caught on immediately, clapping his hands and laughing. "It's me, Grammy," he said. "You forgot me." The entrance into his classroom started on a high note and he often asks me to play the "Forgetting game."

It's okay to be silly with little ones, as long as you don't talk down to them.

Bring humor into your lives. Take home funny videos for the family to watch together. Talk with the kids about the different forms of comedy, from Charlie Chaplin to The Three Stooges to the more cerebral humor of Jerry Seinfeld and Woody Allen. Cut out cartoons from magazines and newspapers and put them on your refrigerator or paste them into a scrapbook. Buy humor books and have a contest to see who in the family can tell the funniest joke. Encourage laughter at your family table. Comedian Bob Hope expressed the power of laughter by saying, "Maybe if we could all laugh alike, and laugh at the same time, this world of ours wouldn't be able to find so many things to squabble about." The same is true when you are blending families. Laughter can become your family's common language.

SPOUSES NEED TO PLAN FOR ONE-ON-ONE TIME TOGETHER, TOO

Sometimes planning time for you and your spouse alone together is like writing a message on a postcard: There's often no room to add anything more. But when you become aware of the need for stronger communication—not only for the good of your marriage, but also for the good of your children—you should be able to reassess your priorities and help each other to make a stronger commitment to that personal time.

Sadly, one-on-one time with your spouse is often the first resolution that gets tossed aside when the frantic pace of work and coping with your blended family takes over. Don't let that happen. You're too important. Your marriage is the foundation on which this new family is built. Take that responsibility seriously.

> Sean and Molly have a standing Friday night date. That's the night her son goes to live with his biological father for three nights. Now that they're expecting a child of their own, they've already agreed to have a regular sitter come in that night. "We've grown to love our special date night," Sean said. "Sometimes we use it to discuss issues we haven't had a chance to cover before. We're a two-career family and I often have to work weekends. Usually, though, our Friday night is a romantic evening, one we have fun planning together."

Whatever you determine as your private time together, be sure it's uninterrupted time. Turn off the television. Let the answering machine pick up your phone calls. Go walking together if the kids are old enough to leave alone. Communication, like sex, works best when you both make time for it and just don't wait for it to "happen."

▪ KNOW WHEN TO KEEP YOUR MOUTH SHUT ▪

As important as it is to make time for communication, sometimes it's the better part of valor to keep your mouth shut. The old saying, "Sticks and stones can break my bones, but words can never harm me," is inaccurate. Words *can* harm you and your relationship—with your new spouse, your kids and stepkids, your former spouse, and the in-laws and ex-in-laws by the dozens. Author Robert Fulghum said it best when he wrote, "Sticks and stones may break my bones, but words will break our hearts." And he is right.

Although you can retract or apologize for words said aloud in haste or anger, they can't be unheard or, unfortunately, easily forgotten. A judge may instruct a jury to "disregard" certain comments during a trial, but the lawyers on both sides know that although a jury may try to disregard, they may easily remember those comments when it's time for deliberation in the jury room.

THINK BEFORE YOU SPEAK WHEN ANGER AND OTHER EMOTIONS ARE IN THE AIR

Give yourself time to compose your words carefully when you are angry or otherwise under great emotional strain or when someone is angry or frustrated with you. A stepmother wisely kept her mouth shut when, after asking her stepdaughter how cheerleading tryouts went, the teenager snapped back, "It's none of your business. I hate you. You're not my mother. You just hope I did lousy. Well, I did. I hope you're satisfied."

"I can hear how frustrated you are," the stepmother finally answered quietly. "I'm sorry. It must have been very disappointing."

The youngster broke into tears and, sobbing, told her stepmother how sad she felt. The women simply put her arm around her stepdaughter and silently comforted her. Think how different this scenario could have been if the stepmother had responded to her stepdaughter's outburst by saying, "I hate you too. I'm *glad* I'm not your mother."

STEPPARENT AS THE MEDIATOR

Often the stepparent finds him or herself sitting on the bench during a squabble between the spouse and the stepkids, when neither party is communicating because no one is listening. Stay out of the fray when emotions are high, unless you are called into play. At that point, you may suddenly find yourself in the role of mediator between your spouse and his or her kids. You can be more objective because you have less emotional involvement and don't share the past history. Don't pick sides, though. A family circle has no sides. Get your spouse and stepchild to stop talking at each other long enough to listen to what you have observed.

If you think your spouse was unfair or handled a particular situation poorly, don't correct him or her in front of the kids. Wait until you're alone together, then tactfully suggest how things could have been handled differently. All parents need to present a united front to the children. When you're blending families, it's even more important to do so to prevent his kids and your kids from taking sides.

DON'T SPEAK UNTIL YOU'VE GATHERED ALL THE FACTS

When my kids were teenagers and had stayed out past curfew, I often was waiting by the door, thankful that they weren't lying bloody on the interstate somewhere, but ready to jump all over them for being late. After one such display of frustration and anger, when it turned out the battery had died right when they were on the highway and they had no way to call us, I learned to bite my tongue and get the facts first. Usually, but not always, there was a good reason why they were late. In those other cases, I quickly discovered that I could drive them crazy by being perfectly calm and rational . . . as I grounded them.

In his book, *The 7 Habits of Highly Effective Families*, the author Stephen R. Covey relates a father's story of how his wife waited to get the facts before she reacted to her son's behavior.

"I came home from work the other day, and my three-and-a-half-year-old son Brenton met me at the door. He was beaming. He said, "Dad, I am a hardworking man!"

"I later found out that while my wife had been downstairs, Brenton had emptied a one-and-a-half gallon jug of water from the fridge, most of it on the floor. My wife's initial reaction had been to yell at him and spank him. But instead she stopped herself and said patiently. "Brenton, what were you trying to do?"

"I was trying to be a helping man, Mom," he replied proudly.

"What do you mean?" she asked.

"I washed the dishes for you."

Sure enough, there on the kitchen table were all the dishes he had washed with the water from the water jug.

"Well, honey, why did you use the water from the fridge?"

"I couldn't reach the water in the sink."

"Oh," she said. Then she looked around. "Well, what do you think you could do next time that would make less of a mess?"

He thought about it for a minute. Then his face lit up. "I could do it in the bathroom!" he exclaimed.

"The dishes might break in the bathroom," she replied. "But how about this? What if you came and got me and I helped you move a chair in front of the kitchen sink so that you could do the work there?"

"Good idea," he exclaimed happily.

"Now, what should we do with this mess?" she asked.

"Well," he said thoughtfully, "we could use a lot of paper towels!" So she gave him some paper towels, and she went and got the mop.

As she was telling me what had happened, I realized how important it was that my wife had been able to catch herself between stimulus and response. She made a proactive choice. And she was able to do it because she thought about the end in mind. The important thing here is not having a clean floor. It's raising this boy.

It took her about ten minutes to clean up the mess. If she had been reactive, it also would have taken her about ten minutes, but the difference would have been that Brenton would have met me at the door and said, "Daddy, I am a bad boy." (pp. 70-71)

(From *The Seven Habits of Highly Effective Families* by Stephen R. Covey. Copyright © 1997 by Franklin Covey Company. Published by Golden Books Publishing Company Inc. All rights reserved. Used by permission.)

DON'T TELL TALES OUT OF SCHOOL

Finally you've achieved what you wanted. The stepkids have opened up to you, sharing some bit of themselves. Treat these tidbits like the treasures they are. Don't betray the youngsters' trust by telling what you've heard, unless, of course, it is something potentially dangerous to their well-being. You may think it's cute that your ten-year-old stepson admitted to you that he has a heart-throb in his fifth grade class, but if he overhears you telling the older kids or your best friend on the telephone, it will be a long time before he trusts you with a confidence again.

Respect your spouse's confidences, too. Pillow talk is just that, and should stay between the two of you. Contrary to what most people think, women are more likely to tell tales out of school, not men. If something funny happened between the two of you, ask your spouse if he or she minds your sharing it with others. Then respect that decision.

▪ HOLD REGULAR FAMILY MEETINGS ▪

Families should not be pure democracies; they *can*, however, be benign dictatorships. What I mean by this is that parents, as the adults, must assume leadership of the family unit. It shows that the biological parent and the stepparent are (hopefully) on the same page and gives credibility to the stepparent's role of an equal partner. While it's vital to be open to input from the children, especially as they grow into their preteen and teen years, the parents must be responsible for final decisions that ultimately affect the entire family.

This philosophy may present difficulties for the blended family. Before the remarriage, the single parent often may have relied heavily on input and advice from his or her children. "You're the man of the family now . . ." or "You're going to have to help run the house now. You're the woman in charge" gives children an unfair and heavy burden to carry, yet surprisingly, it is one that they may be reluctant to lay down once their parent has remarried.

One way to gather opinions and let all members of the family feel as though they have a say in matters pertaining to them is through regularly scheduled family meetings. Youngsters like having rules and regulations spelled out for them and are more likely to be compliant when they have had input in making these decisions.

THE PURPOSE OF FAMILY MEETINGS IS TO CREATE A SAFE OPEN FORUM

Our family's been holding regular meetings since our children first started school. Each fall they would bring their allowance requests in writing, showing how the money was to be budgeted and why they (always) needed more than the year before. We'd discuss pertinent issues such as how household chores would be assigned, whether we should get another dog or cat, where to go on the next family vacation, and as they grew older, curfews and use of the family car. Now they're all adults, yet we still have Sunday night dinners together with whoever is able to attend. We still talk about family issues, including who wants to use the football tickets, who can feed someone's cats during a vacation period, and just general catching up. As one of my kids (over thirty, but then one's children are always "kids," regardless of the age) said about family meetings, "It's a great way to get everyone's input. Often it becomes a creative brainstorming session, just like we have in our workplace."

Setting up family meetings may be more difficult in blended families because the youngsters haven't grown up with the idea. It's something you're foisting on them that seems new and possibly awkward, especially if the children are adolescents. Call it a "family council" or "forum" if "family meeting" sounds too formal. Explain that its purpose is to become an arena for a safe open exchange of ideas, airing of complaints, and discussion of issues that confront the family. Even if communication skills within your family are not yet strong, the fact that you are providing an opportunity for self-expression should lower some defenses and open some doors.

Parents often make decisions arbitrarily and too rapidly, without really thinking them through. The group discussion that develops in a family meeting helps to slow down the process and sharpen the focus. These family meetings also give you an important perspective concerning the other side of an issue. As the youngsters become more comfortable with the format and realize that they won't be criticized or ridiculed by expressing their concerns, they'll open up more. This allows you to better understand what your children are really thinking, how they feel about sharing their home with a new stepparent and, possibly, new stepsiblings, where the pinch points are, and what solutions can be devised. If a new baby will soon arrive on the scene, family meetings are a good place to discuss what changes will occur in the family, how baby-sitting chores will be handled, and what "our baby" means to everyone.

Family meetings give youngsters a feeling of being empowered. They not only learn to stand up for their rights, but they also learn the art of compromise. Kids quickly discover how to express themselves concisely and effectively. They receive positive feedback about their judgment and creative thinking ability and learn responsibility. These are valuable assets in helping a young person to feel confident and to raise his or her self-esteem.[2]

A recent study of adolescents published in the September 10, 1997, issue of the *Journal of the American Medical Association* concluded that feelings of warmth, being loved and understood, and paid attention to by parents help teenagers avoid high-risk activities such as drug use, alcohol use, attempted suicide, or becoming sexually active at an early age, regardless of whether a child comes from a one- or two-parent household. The study went on to say that this emotional attachment also was more important in protecting teenagers than the amount of time parents spend at home. Certainly, the family meetings can play a vital role in achieving this important parent-family connectedness.

To be candid, at times it seemed as though not much actually took place at some of our meetings and I wondered if they had been worthwhile. Years later, however, my children confided that they felt the fact that we had held the family meetings showed

---

[2]Elaine Fantle Shimberg, *Depression: What Families Should Know* (New York, 1991), Ballantine Books.

them how much importance we placed on the family as a unit. It strengthened their sense of belonging, even when they experienced the usual emotional upheavals all young people encounter.

HOW TO ORGANIZE A FAMILY MEETING

1. Schedule a specific date and time so everyone knows when it is to be held, such as the first Sunday of every month at 7:00 p.m.

Although some experts suggest meeting on a weekly basis, I think that would be overkill and may diminish its significance. You can always call a special meeting if there's a reason for it.

2. Attendance is required.

Be sure to include the children who live with you only part of the week or during summer or other school vacation times. While the rules at their other home may be different, they need to be involved in making those to be enforced at yours.

Even if one of the youngsters thinks a family meeting is a dumb idea and sits away from the others, acting bored and disinterested, don't be concerned. He or she will be eavesdropping and eventually should begin to take part.

3. Extra meetings may be called by anyone's request.

4. The meeting will be conducted by one of the parents (usually the biological parent), but everyone will have the opportunity to speak on every issue.

5. The meeting will be taped (or have someone take notes) in case there are questions later about what took place and what decisions were made.

6. Complete honesty is encouraged, although no one may interrupt, shout, or display any lack of courtesy to others.

7. Innovative suggestions and creative thought are encouraged.

8. Decisions will be made on a majority basis, although the parents will maintain the right to a veto when deemed necessary (such as a family trip to Europe or getting a new pet).

ENCOURAGE EVERYONE'S INPUT IN CREATING AN AGENDA

Having a written agenda that is handed out to everyone the day before the family meeting not only gives family members a chance to think about issues, but it also serves to underline the importance of these meetings.

What goes into an agenda will become personalized to your family needs. For a start you may want to list:

- Old business that needs to be acted upon or at least discussed
- New business
- Good and welfare
- Suggestions

Some blended families create a suggestion box in the kitchen where family members can drop notes with gripes, compliments, or just ideas to be discussed anonymously. This may offer a higher comfort level for youngsters just getting to know each other as stepsiblings.

Remember that each blended family is unique. What works for one family may not work for you. Be patient and be willing to experiment. Listen to the children's ideas for creative ways to work through potential problems. The good news is that by remaining open to new ideas for solutions, you and your family will be on your way to improving communication skills, as well as becoming a more unified family unit.

▪ COMMUNICATION SKILLS CAN BE LEARNED ▪

Don't despair if your attempts at improving communication in your blended family seem destined for failure. Keep working at it. Make the effort to begin today. Talk more, communicate through touch, share your thoughts and feelings even just a little bit more than yesterday. Unspoken resentment can build on itself, feeding and growing like a cancer until it destroys the family life you're trying to create. When your spouse and children see you making the effort to become a better communicator, you'll be giving them permission to open up just a little bit more themselves. Communication skills *can* be learned. You can improve yours and help your family improve theirs by putting into practice some of the suggestions found in this chapter.

CHAPTER FOUR

Dealing with a Former Spouse

"Among well-bred people, a mutual deference is affected; contempt of others disguised; authority concealed; attention given to each in his turn; and an easy stream of conversation is maintained, without vehemence, without interruption, without eagerness for victory, and without any airs of superiority."

—DAVID HUME,
Scottish philosopher & historian
1711–1776

When you first divorce, you may wish that your former spouse would disappear from the face of the earth so you wouldn't ever have to deal with him/her again. But you shouldn't get your wish. Although the two of you have ended the "for better or for worse" part of your marriage, your parenthood is "until death do you part." You may have divorced one another, but you can't divorce your kids. Your relationship will endure even if your ex-spouse (ES) has died or disappeared.

You also may not want to divorce the other relatives that you acquired with your former spouse. Many divorced couples still enjoy their relationship with their former spouse's sister, work with the ex-spouse's brother, or want to maintain the children's connection with their former in-laws, their kids' grandparents, even though they understand that a former spouse's parents probably are supportive of their own adult child.

The majority of divorced parents are able to mask or even put their ill feelings, resentments, and bitterness behind them on issues pertaining to the well-being of their children. But for numerous others, every joint decision—both major and minor—becomes an ugly struggle. It's a seemingly impossible situation when you're supposed to communicate and compromise with someone with whom you're unable to stay married.

"We keep in fairly regular contact with both my husband's and my kids' other parents," said a woman who was both a divorced mother and stepmother. "It's imperative for me to have as good a relationship as I can with my ex and my husband's ex for the sake of the kids. Sometimes it takes all my strength (and then some) to be kind and diplomatic. But it has proven well worth the effort when you see how positive an impact it has on the kids for their parents NOT to be at war—and not to be used as spies or weapons between the houses. It takes a great burden off the kids not to have to choose and switch sides twice a week."

Then she added, "Right now Alan's dad and I are working "together" to help our son, Alan (age eight), to overcome some feelings of being unimportant and left out, and not being loved enough. He *is* important and loved, and is included, but he doesn't "feel" it. So that's a nice thing about getting along. You can work together for the best of your child instead of fighting."

Usually this "truce" doesn't come naturally. There's bound to be anger and bitterness, and something akin to hatred, especially if you didn't want the divorce and your ES did or if your ES really did you wrong in many ways. But time and focusing on what a working relationship can mean to your kids often pays dividends.

"My ex-husband's new wife hated me from the start," Nicole said. "Why, I don't know. But she'd never answer the phone when I'd call to talk to my daughter when it was her turn to stay with her dad. If there were an event at school, his wife wouldn't come if she thought I'd be there too, which of course, I was. Then, about five years after she and my ex married, I got remarried too. A year later, I got pregnant and learned that she also was. To my surprise, she answered the phone the next time I called and was quite chatty, asking me how I was feeling and describing her symptoms. The next time there was a field trip at school, she and I both ended up being chaperones. Again, she was friendly and seemed relax. I could see my daughter's relief when she observed how civilized her mother and stepmother finally were. I guess time just took care of things."

• DON'T LET THE KIDS CONQUER AND DIVIDE •

Kids often are the real perpetrators in the continuing war between their divorced parents. They hang onto the thought that their parents might get back together if they could only ruin the credibility of the stepparent. They often create fantasies, conjuring up plots that put them in control.

It isn't just with divorced parents, either. All kids test their parents. You're no different. With their computers as with their parents/stepparents, kids quickly learn what buttons to push to get the desired results. One of the benefits of the adults in the youngster's two houses keeping open the lines of communication is that they can check facts with one another, and not let the kids fictionalize events.

"The stories my stepdaughter, a teenager, made up about me still leave me speechless. Her dad wouldn't believe his daughter would tell such stories and looked the other way. At the same time, I used to cry every time Sally left our house because she told me almost equally bad stories about the abuses she suffered at her mom's and stepfather's house. About two years ago, it all came to a head.

"She told her mom that I only bought her cheap clothes, that I stole the expensive shampoo her mother sent over and gave it to my son, and that I never spent anything on her. I finally made her mom sit down with me and told her the real story about all she heard. We both shared information that shocked the other and were both hurt and surprised. Then we called Sally in and discussed it with her. We told her that we'd keep closer contact with each other and forbid her to make up stories that hurt other people.

It's gotten better. Her father and I don't allow her to say anything negative about her mom or stepfather here, although she says (if I can

believe her), that she's still trashing me at her mom's house. I think she
was just trying to get attention through her lies. And it worked. She got
the attention of all four of the adults in her life. But now she knows
that we'll check with each other before we believe the worst."

▪ BE AWARE OF YOUR MOTIVATION ▪

Ask yourself if your driving motivation when meeting with your
ES is a power play, control, or an honest desire to do what's best
for your children.

To best answer this, you need to search within yourself. Explain your motives to yourself, then honestly critique your answer
being as objective as you can. Are you trying to show your ES
"who's boss?" Are you being stubborn because last time there was
a decision to make your ES "won" the argument, so this time it's
your turn? Are you trying to save face with your new spouse to
prove that you're not a pushover?

Look instead within your heart. Release the negative emotions
of anger, bitterness, jealousy, and resentment. What really is the
best decision for your child's well-being? If you were still married
to the youngster's other parent, what would you have decided together? Why is this conclusion different?

▪ ACKNOWLEDGE THE PRESENCE AND IMPORTANCE ▪
OF YOUR EX-SPOUSE IN YOUR CHILD'S LIFE

Many divorced parents emotionally deny the existence of the
ES until decisions have to be made. Then there is no relationship
on which to build; it's like negotiating with a total stranger.

I know from first-hand experience what this is like. My son
began dating Joshua's mother when my grandson was almost
three. As the relationship became more serious, I began spending
one-on-one time with my future grandson, albeit a step-grandson.
I subconsciously blurred any thought of his father and focused
instead on my son's future life as Joshua's stepfather.

When Joshua was four, I had taken him to the aquarium one day and was driving home, trying to remember which streets were one-way this week. He chattered from the backseat. Finally I said, "Joshua, you'll have to be quiet a minute. Grammy's trying to drive and I need to concentrate. I don't want to get in an accident. I've got precious cargo here."

Predictably, he asked, "What's precious cargo?"

"You are," I answered. "It means I love you and don't want you to get hurt."

"You love me?" he repeated. I nodded. "Who else loves me?"

"Your grandfather loves you," I said, "and your mommy loves you, Scott (my son) loves you . . ." I added all my other children's names to the love list. Then I hesitated, almost in surprise at my obvious omission. "And your daddy loves you," I finished.

I was shaken at my subconscious denial to add his biological father's name to my list. I had never verbalized it, but it was there anyway. From that day on I accepted the fact that my grandson loves and is loved by many people, including his mother and my son, who is his stepfather, but also including his father.

If you're the biological parent who has remarried, you may need to help your new parents-in-law by giving them permission to acknowledge your ES as an important part of your child's life. They don't have to like your ES any more than you do, but the relationship should be respected for the benefit of your child, their new grandchild.

▪ ENCOURAGE CIVILITY BETWEEN THE STEPPARENT ▪
AND THE SAME SEX EX-SPOUSE

In addition to building a coalition with a former spouse, the biological parent who has remarried needs to be sensitive to the feelings of the stepparent. In divorces without children involved, two adults marry and hopefully, live happily ever after, seldom thinking about the past. When children are involved, however, the past is always present, not only in the form of the children, but also the ES.

Even the most secure adult can begin to resent regular meetings and nighttime phone calls from a mate's ES, even if the conference addresses concerns about the biological parents' child. While jealousy may not be an admitted issue, the fact that the parents once were married and that they share a common history with the child may make the stepparent feel like an outsider at times.

> "My ex-husband and present husband don't tend to talk unless they have to," the mother of a seven-year-old said. "Not because there are bad feelings, but because they both are a little uncomfortable. They just let me run the middle. Most stuff is handled over the phone or when my son's dad comes to get him." She added thoughtfully, "With my husband's daughter, Kathy, it's different. My husband's ex-wife and her husband tend to meet us for lunch to discuss things. That way everyone can be a part and it's easier than over the phone. We also know who has what to say and there is less game playing, name calling, and accusations if we're in disagreement. Kathy's stepdad is pretty reasonable and is easier to talk to than her mother."

NEVER CRITICIZE YOUR STEPCHILDREN'S SAME SEX BIOLOGICAL PARENT TO THEM

Regardless how frustrated a stepparent may feel concerning the lack of responsibility or failures of the same-sex biological parent, mum's the word. Bite your tongue, if you have to. Write your complaints down on paper, then shred the paper. Type them on your computer, then delete your words.

Never criticize your stepchildren's same sex biological parent to them either. Even if they know what you say is true, they'll never forgive you for mentioning it. What's worse, they'll hold it against you. It can negatively impact your relationship with your stepchildren. Don't do it.

▪ AGREE ON AND SET GUIDELINES ▪

Before a mediator or negotiator begins work, he or she sets up rules that both sides must sign off on. You and your ES must do the same or you'll make life far more difficult than it needs to be. Some of the guidelines include:

1. Have a definite time period and a convenient neutral place to meet, such as a restaurant or park, to discuss issues concerning your children.

2. Be on time and don't cancel unless absolutely necessary.

3. Notify one another before the meeting what issues need to be discussed.

4. Stick to those issues.

5. Do not bring up past history.

6. Agree to and maintain fair fighting rules, including no shouting or name calling.

7. Avoid expecting your ES to read your mind.

8. Practice active listening skills (see Chapter 3), even if you can't stand the sound of your ES's voice.

9. Verbalize the action that will be taken and by whom. Put it in writing and date it so there's no question of the decision at a later time.

For some ESs, it is too painful to even be in the same room with one another, let alone contemplate meeting one-on-one in a civilized manner. These individuals may find that the telephone, letters, or even e-mail can provide the necessary "safe" distance for them to make decisions. Others have found it beneficial to let the stepparent spouses, who may be more objective, meet for them, although I personally feel this is abdicating responsibility for the children. These latter parents could benefit from working with a capable counselor or therapist to help them overcome their debilitating emotions.

▪ KEEP ON POINT ▪

One of the biggest detriments in dealing with joint decisions is falling from point—bringing in side issues (often old ones from the former marriage) that have no bearing on the resolution at hand. Often the stepparent or grandparent is standing on the sidelines, feeding the fire and forcing the spouse to make decisions that please the stepparent or grandparent, rather than focusing on what is best for his or her child.

Be alert for these skid areas on the track and stay on the main road. There's a purpose for your trip; don't forget your final destination is to do the best for your children. Come up with a cue word, such as "slipping," or "detour" that either of you can use when you detect that either of you are wobbling.

▪ HOW TO RESOLVE IRRESOLVABLE ISSUES ▪

WORK IT OUT AS RESPONSIBLE ADULTS

Sometimes the anger and bitterness between two former spouses is so strong that it makes one or both of them act like children. Two parents with joint custody were notified by their child's elementary school principal that both the classroom teacher and guidance counselor thought their youngster would benefit from joining the school's "children of divorce" group. During these sessions, the children could openly discuss feelings and how they handled specific situations. The mother readily agreed. The father refused his permission.

"After trying in vain to gain consent," the principal said, "I realized it was time for me to withdraw and charge them with the responsibility—their responsibility as parents—to their child. I told them that they had two weeks to work out this issue like mature adults and come back to me. The father finally agreed, but with the caveat that the child could attend these sessions only for a restricted period of time."

MEET WITH AN IMPARTIAL COUNSELOR

If you can't seem to decide on even the most basic of decisions concerning your children, you and your ES should meet with an impartial counselor. It can be a trained member of the clergy, guidance counselor, a social worker, psychologist, or psychiatrist. Your child needs both parents to be supportive; try to put your differences behind and focus ahead to your child's future.

USE THE COURTS AS A LAST RESORT

Although they are overcrowded, the courts are available to solve problems that parents are unable or unwilling to work out themselves. It will cost you more in terms of money, time, and emotional stress. Use the judicial system only as a last resort.

▪ YOUR EX-SPOUSE IS IN YOUR LIFE FOREVER ▪
WHEN YOU HAVE KIDS

You might as well get used to working with and compromising with your ES now. You're in it together for the long haul whether you like it or not. If you don't start to work together now, it won't get easier as time goes on.

There are numerous decisions that must be made while your children are still minors, ranging from which Little League team to join (in your neighborhood or your ES's neighborhood) to choice of schools, medical needs, and college selection. Even once the kids are grown you'll have to "put on a happy face" and appear together for graduations, weddings, baptisms, namings, and other life cycle events.

You don't have to go as far as one of the couples I interviewed, in which all four of the adults socialize together. But you do need to make the extra effort to be civil to your ES, so your joint children won't have to keep stealing looks across the room to see if Mom and Dad are behaving themselves this time.

CHAPTER FIVE

Home Is Where the Kids Are

"It was the policy of the good old gentleman to make his children feel that home was the happiest place in the world; and I value this delicious home-feeling as one of the choicest gifts a parent can bestow."

—WASHINGTON IRVING

For many stepchildren, the definition of "home" depends on which "home" is being described. "Mom's home" may be a two-story brick colonial with a fireplace in the family room, a basement, and a fenced-in backyard with room for the three dogs to roam. "Daddy's home" may be a one-story frame house, with a giant television screen in the family room, and a swimming pool in the backyard. Or, depending on finances, Mom's home may be a small three-bedroom, one-bathroom home with two sets of bunk beds in two of the bedrooms for her kids and her new husband's kids. Dad's place might be a one-bedroom apartment with a pull-out couch for the kids to use when it's his turn to have them. How well these tumbleweed kids roll from one home to the other—emotionally as well as physically—depends largely on the adjustments, flexibility, and compromises made by their parents and stepparents.

During summer and school holidays you'll find children of all ages flocking to airports, bus terminals, and train depots like the swallows returning to Capistrano, as they make their way across the country to visit their "other" parent. For many kids, however, the move is merely a matter of traveling across town or even walking around the block. Whether you're the one seeing them off or the one getting your house in order for the anticipated "company," there are many specific ways to make this shift run more smoothly.

■ WHEN YOU'RE THE ONE SAYING "GOOD-BYE" ■

Despite the fact that you may rather have root canal work done than send your darlings off to your ES and "that woman" or "that man," it's your job to make the exchange run smoothly for your youngsters. They already may be feeling a little uneasy about leaving you, or somewhat anxious about the anticipated welcome at the other end. As kids often take their cue from their parents, don't make the departure any worse for them by tossing in your negative attitude, leftover bitterness, or residual anger at your ES. You'll only be adding additional anxiety in a possibly stressful situation.

Whether the trip is across town or across the country, these suggestions can ease the way:

· Make the travel arrangements in cooperation with your ES.

Do not put your kids in the middle. Unless your kids are teenagers who prefer to make their own arrangements, you check the time and place of pick-up with your ES, rather than relying on your kids' memory. If you're sending your kids on a bus, train, or plane, be certain that your ES or another relative knows when they're coming and where to meet the youngsters—at the gate or the baggage area. Most airlines will not release a minor unless the predetermined adult is there at the gate to pick the child up.

· Let younger children know how long they'll be away.

Younger children have little sense of time, so even a week away can seem like an eternity. To help them keep track of the days, make a calendar showing the date of departure and the date of return. Put special stickers on the days you'll be calling and then be sure you make that call.

· Use a felt-tipped marker on a city, state, or country map to show your kids exactly where they'll be going.

Don't assume your older children are knowledgeable about geography either. They may think Iowa, Ohio, and Idaho are all the same state. (I've known adults who thought that, too.) If your kids are going to a major city, such as Chicago, New York, Philadelphia, a coastal village, or farm, check the bookstore or your library for age appropriate books about the area. Robert McCloskey's *Blueberries for Sal*, for example, is a wonderful book for younger children that describes gathering blueberries in Maine. *Lady in the Box*, by Ann McGovern, deals with the homeless in a major city. There are numerous others you can consider. For older kids, collect some of the many available travel books that focus on the area to which they'll be going. Travel agencies and AAA often have a variety of books about a particular area. If you write away for information, put it in the kids' names so they can get the mail.

· Pack a variety of clothes, depending on the weather and activities being planned.

Ask your ES to let you know what activities are being planned so your kids can come prepared. If you live in the South and your kids are headed north, you may not be able to get warm clothing for them. Discuss that ahead of time with your ES so he or she can line up the proper outfits. If the kids are heading south, be sure to tuck in a sweater or jacket, even if the trip is to Florida in the summer. Air conditioning can be downright cold at times.

Avoid last-minute confrontations with your ES such as, "I sent you the money. Why haven't you bought the clothes for the kids?" Work your financial details out ahead of time, so you're not sending the kids off to their other parent or receiving them with hostility vibes still in the air. Kids are extremely attuned to negativity between their parents.

· Include a favorite book or toy and a copy of a photo of yourself with your children.

Don't send the original picture or use an expensive or favorite frame. If it's forgotten, you may not get it back. If you're on the receiving end of the kids, don't stick the picture in a drawer or back in the suitcase. Remember that regardless how excited the kids are to see you, they probably feel a little guilty leaving their other parent (as well as stepsibs and/or half brothers and sisters) back home. The photo may help alleviate that anxiety. Remember to pack up the favorite toy, book, or yes, that picture too, when the kids go home.

· Be sure your ex-spouse knows your younger children's special bedtime routines.

Make things go more smoothly for your commuter youngster by reminding your ES of special routines, especially at bedtime. Kids get very rigid when it comes to these comfort rituals, such as the number of books read before bedtime, a night-light being on, and the door either open or shut at bedtime. Don't expect your child's other parent to remember the routine if he or she only sees the youngster a few weeks out of the year. Remember too that last year's rituals may be obsolete this year, so prepare your ES for the updated operating procedure.

· Be sure to alert your ex-spouse to any new allergies to food, medications, or insect bites.

Children can develop new allergies quickly. For your child's well-being, be sure to tell the other parent of any allergies that may have cropped up since the last time your youngster was there.

· Send detailed information concerning any medication being taken, along with an extra pair of glasses or contacts, and written instructions on various orthodontic paraphernalia.

Don't expect your ES to remember oral instructions over the phone and don't trust your kids to remember either. Write all medical information down. If your handwriting's not great, type or print the facts clearly.

· Put on a happy face and don't burden your children with a recitation of how lonely you'll be until their return.

Try to hold back tears until the train or plane leaves. While it's all right to tell the children you'll be thinking of them, don't sigh or say how lonely you'll be. Chances are they already feel a little guilty about leaving you as it is.

· On the other hand, don't go overboard by listing all the wonderful, fun things you have planned during your children's absence, especially if you and your new spouse have "our" children (or his) who will be with you.

Having your spouse's kids coming to live with you and your mutual kids while your kids by your ES go to see their other parent is a little like an English farce, with people coming and going and doors opening and slamming shut. Obviously, you want to show your stepchildren a good time while they're with you, but if the period overlaps when your other kids are away, hold back on the descriptions of all the great fun you'll be having.

· Don't undergo any major changes during your child's absence, such as getting remarried; divorced, if you have remarried; adopting a child; or moving.

· Don't redecorate your children's rooms in their absence. You may think it will be a great surprise when they return; chances are *they'll* think you've intruded on their privacy (and you've probably thrown out some piece of "junk" that they treasured.)

Transportation Tips[1]

- If your children will be traveling alone, contact the airlines, bus company, or train company to learn what their requirements are concerning age and safety factors.

- Before your children leave, arrange for each of them to have a telephone calling card and be sure they know how to make a long distance call. Prepare a list of emergency telephone numbers, including your home, work, and cell phone as well as those of your ES.

- Select a direct route, if possible. If there are connections, be sure your youngsters know what to do, where to go, and with whom it is safe to go.

- Let each child select small toys, books, and games for his or her travel backpack. You can add a surprise, but don't enclose a mushy note saying how much you'll miss your kid.

- If your children are flying, check to see if you can order special children's meals. If not, pack a lunch bag with nonperishable favorite lunch foods.

- To minimize the risk of kidnapping, establish a code word or phrase to be used in case your ES is delayed at the other end and an unexpected stranger must pick up your children upon their arrival at their destination. Instruct your children to refuse to go with anyone who doesn't know the word or phrase, even if it's someone in uniform.

■ WHEN YOU'RE THE ONE SAYING "HELLO" ■

There's stress involved when you're on the receiving end of getting the kids, as well. If you're the parent whose turn it is to have the kids, you want everything to be "perfect," forgetting that

---

[1]Some of these suggestions are taken from *Coping with Kids and Vacation*, by Linda Albert and Elaine Fantle Shimberg (New York, 1986), Ballantine Books.

life—especially life with kids—usually isn't. If you're the stepparent, you're faced with a weekend, weeks, holiday, or an entire summer with children you may not have had much time to really get to know too well. You also are fully aware that your spouse, the kids' parent, may be uptight and not have too much time to spend with you. There's little doubt that it's going to be a stressful time. (See Chapter Thirteen for ways to help reduce stress.)

One way to ease the transition is to say the kids are "living with us this summer" or "over Christmas," rather than using the word, "visiting." Our perception of things becomes our reality. When we say the stepchildren are "visiting," we begin to treat them like visitors or guests and, unconsciously, invite them to think of themselves that way. Visitors or guests are not asked to do chores around the house. We don't make them follow "house rules." Usually, we think of ways to entertain them. And that can be exhausting—to us as well as to the kids who probably aren't used to having every minute of their lives crammed full of activities, no matter how wonderful they may be.

When we treat our children/stepchildren as guests, rather than our kids, we reinforce their feeling of not really belonging to this family.

"My brother and I spent weekends with my father after my parent's divorce when I was three," an almost thirty-year-old man recalled. "When he remarried, his wife was insistent that neither my brother nor I should have a key to 'her' house, despite the fact that we were in our teens and wanted to go out with friends at night. It made me wonder if we were really welcome there at all. I often still wonder why my father, now deceased, didn't stand up for us more."

If there are other children in the family, either stepsiblings or kids from the new marriage, these "permanent" youngsters may resent having to do chores while their "visiting" stepsiblings or half-siblings are given the guest treatment. This may create an undercurrent of hostility that can prevent a bettering of relationships within the family.

GIVE ALL THE KIDS RESPONSIBILITIES

While the children/stepchildren are living with you, make them feel at home by giving them their fair share of the household chores. Although they may grumble about having to groom the dog or taking a turn to haul the trash out to the street, they'll feel like they belong to this family, even if it's only on a short-term basis.

Establish the same age-appropriate rules for these children as you have for those kids living with you full-time. If your other kids have to clear the table and take turns doing the dishes, add them to the roster. If two hours of television viewing is the limit, apply it across the board. If your own teenagers have to be in by 11:30 p.m., they must too.

You may run into problems, however, if the teenagers curfew at their other house is significantly later than the one established at your home. That's when family meetings and open communication can help. Be aware that you obviously will have to arrive at some type of compromise, one of which will affect your full-time teens as well. Once agreed upon, make sure that all the kids follow the agreed upon curfew. If they refuse to fulfill their obligations, have them experience the same punishment as your other kids would.

It usually works better to have the children's biological parent hand out assignments to his or her kids when they're living with you. On the other hand, if the work detail is given out during family meetings, it's a good opportunity to let the tumbleweed kids feel that they're part of this family group, which they are, even if it's only on a part-time basis.

WHAT ABOUT GUILT?

A biological parent, who only has his or her kids for a short time, is bound to feel guilty saying "no" or making a fuss over the kids having to take out the garbage. "They're only here for such a short time," is the usual rationalization. But in the long run, you make the children feel more welcomed by including them, not only in the fun activities, but also in the everyday activities that make a group of individuals into a family and help a home to run effectively. Responsibilities may differ from one home to the other, and usually they do. It doesn't mean that one way is right and the other wrong, only that they are different in different homes. But to deprive youngsters from sharing in some responsibilities is to reinforce their self-image as a being merely a visitor in one of their parent's homes.

WHERE SHOULD THEY STAY?

The ideal, of course, would be to have special permanent bedrooms (in the west wing?) set aside for each of your kids whenever they come to live with you. Since most of us can't furnish that, however, creativity must be the name of the game.

Some families are fortunate in having a spare bedroom that can be used for the kids living with them part-time. For others, it means shifting their full-time kids around, using trundle beds, futons, bunk beds, or couches that fold out. Sleeping arrangements, however, are not as important as providing a semblance of belonging and of privacy, for your full-time kids as well as the part-time ones. Use this checklist to help make the kids living with you on a short-term basis feel truly at home.

- Popping in to live on a short-term basis in a different home is a lot like coming into a movie somewhere in the middle. It takes a while to figure out what's going on. Give these kids a few hours to get acclimated after they arrive before dragging them off to a whirlwind of activities.

- Assign a dresser, shelf, or closet space to be specifically set aside for the child's things. No one feels at home living out of a suitcase.

- If the children visit on a frequent basis, let them keep personal belongings with you so they don't have to bring them each time. This could mean duplicating some items, such as tooth-brush, jacket, sneakers, and even a sleep toy, although kids usually can tell when you've tried to substitute a look-alike for the real thing.

• Provide a drawer, footlocker, or box with a lock, so the kids feel as though they have a place that's theirs where no one can pry. This is especially important for older children coming into your home where there may be inquisitive toddlers around.

• Accept their need for some time alone, reading on their bed, playing quietly in a corner, or even just sitting on the fence outside, staring into space. If you're the stepparent, don't look at this as a rejection of your company, but rather as an individual's need for privacy.

• Encourage their staying in touch with their other parent by giving them privacy for phone calls or furnishing stationery and postage so they can write. If you have a computer, let them use it for e-mail, but set up some time limits as you do with the use of the telephone.

• Ask their help in planning menus so you can be sure to include some of their favorite foods.

• Plan some time for these kids to be one-on-one just with their biological parent.

• Give them safety information specific to your area of the country, such as shaking out shoes before putting them on if spiders are a problem, using sunscreen in the South, locking doors in more urban areas, and recognizing poisonous plants such as poison oak and poison ivy.

• Write down your phone number and house address and post near every telephone in case of an emergency.

• Don't force your kids to immediately like their stepsiblings or half siblings or expect them to drag these new siblings everywhere they go. Good relationships grow slowly.

· Don't feel you have to deluge the kids with gifts or plan daily entertainment. Instead, give them your attention, your interest, your concern, and your love. That will make them feel more special than doing the Disney World whirl in the long run.

PLAN FOR "ADULT TIME"

Along with all the changes involved when the kids come to live with you for a short time, you may feel there's no time left to squeeze out even a few moments for the two of you grown-ups. The biological parent may be hesitant to steal any of what little precious time there is with the kids for adult time, but feels disloyal to the stepparent for thinking this way. He or she feels torn, anxious, and stressed. Usually, the compromise is to make everything a group activity. But rather than being a good decision, it's one in which everyone feels frustrated. The couple misses their private time and the kids want some time alone with their biological parent. It's important for you to do just that for two reasons.

First of all, you need to schedule time together because it's important for whichever of you is the stepparent to be reassured that you still are an important part of a caring marriage. For both of you to maintain this strong relationship, you must have time to reconnect, communicate, and enjoy each other's company. Otherwise, stress and resentment toward your stepchildren is bound to build. Many stepparents openly admitted that they felt jealousy toward their stepchildren. Usually, such an emotion results from failing to protect the adult time between marriage partners. Chapter Twelve deals strictly with these and other adult issues.

A second and equally important reason that you must have this time to reconnect as adults is that it reinforces to your children the fact that this marriage is strong and that together the two of you are committed to building a secure home for all of your kids. You present a united front. When the biological parent makes clear the distinction between loving his or her children while at the same time having a mature love for the stepparent, most youngsters will be more accepting, even if they still aren't happy about their parent's divorce. Like a drop of water on a roof, however, if they notice the slightest crack, they'll rush in to fill the void.

STAY IN TOUCH

If you live in a different town than your kids, you still can stay in touch when they return to their other home and give them closure on the projects they began with you. Send photos or a videotape showing that the dog likes sleeping in the doghouse they helped build, that the flowers they repotted are still alive, and that the pictures they colored are still on the refrigerator. Use postcards of the local zoo, aquarium, or park or newspaper clippings of local news of interest to let them stay familiar with their "other" community.

Communication is the key, whether your children live with you full-time or whether they are living with you only part of the time. If both natural parents cooperate, rather than compete, children will soon become comfortable with what for them and thousands of other kids is a natural situation—splitting time between Mom's house and Dad's house. As a thirteen-year-old boy admitted, "I've got the best of both worlds—a house in the city and one in the country. My friends think I'm lucky." And indeed he is, because he has parents committed to his well-being.

BE FLEXIBLE

Remember that the only sure things in life are death and taxes. Just because you or your spouse do not have custody of the kids when you marry, doesn't mean that you will never have them. The following two excerpts are examples of what can happen when you least expect it.

"Although my stepson spent time with his dad and me on holidays and summer vacation time, I never expected that we'd have him living with us full-time. His freshman year of college, however, he decided that he really didn't like the school he had chosen and decided to transfer to one near us. Now he's living with us full-time. He's a nice young man and I do like him. It's just that I never expected to have a full-time stepson."

"I've heard quite a few people say that it won't be any big deal [to marry someone with children] because the stepkids won't be around much. But anyone entering into a marriage with children just has to realize that the custody arrangements can change at any time and we all have to be prepared just in case that happens. In my case, my divorced husband did already have custody, but they visited their mother on some weekends and spent eight weeks with her over the summer, so we did get a break now and then. After she was killed, we had them all the time. Even some grown stepkids have been known to move back in with [one of] the parents, so nobody is safe from this."

The moral? Stay flexible. You never know when your kids may decide they'd rather live with you or, if you're a stepparent, that something happens to your spouse's ex. It doesn't have to be a death. The ES may develop a chronic illness and be unable to care for the children. He or she may decide that the responsibility for the kids is just too much and decide to abdicate the parental throne. You'll feel like the Iowa woman who had septuplets, but you won't have the benefit of nine months to get used to the idea. Be forewarned. When you marry someone with kids, never assume that the children won't end up living with you. They just might.

CHAPTER SIX

Discipline

"It is better to bind your children to you by a feeling of respect, and by gentleness, than by fear."

—TERENCE: *ADELPHI* I.i.,
ROMAN PLAYWRIGHT
(185–159 B.C.)

Joining an already established family, as a stepparent must do, is a little like coming in late to an ongoing game of Monopoly. You know how to play the game, but really aren't sure of the local rules. Do they put two hundred dollars in the middle so the player stopping on "Free Parking" gets to keep that along with any fines that have been paid? Are properties auctioned off to the highest bidder when a player needs more money? Can "side deals" be made so a specific player is immune to paying rent two or three times after stopping on a property?

The rules of a household obviously have more serious repercussions, but often they also aren't spelled out to the newcomer. The stepparent may tell the children not to bring food into the living room or drink from the milk bottle, or to make their beds before leaving for school, only to be met with stares and comments of, "We've always done it that way." The bewildered stepparent also may get no reinforcement from the spouse who wonders what the big fuss is all about.

• AGREEING ON VALUES •

Chances are good that the stepparent's first reaction to the spouse's children's discipline is that it has been lax in the past. And probably they're right. Many divorced parents feel that their children have already gone through enough emotional trauma. They delude themselves that they're doing the children a favor by going easy on them, allowing them to run wild through their house, making a mess and breaking things, staying up until they decide to go to bed, saying whatever pops into their head, not picking up after themselves, and becoming unruly at restaurants. The parent excuses such poor behavior with a feeble wave of a hand and by murmuring apologetically, "What can I do?"

> "I know I let my daughter get by with murder," a widow with a six year-old said, "but it was just the two of us. She was just four and was devastated, as I was, when Charles died. I couldn't bear to be tough on her. I didn't want to upset her more. Now that Terry and I are getting married, I hate to change the rules on her. He thinks she's spoiled. I guess he's right..."

That woman's new husband will have his hands full. He'll have to gently guide his wife and reassure her that discipline can be done with love and caring, and that children really do respond to retraining. First, he and his spouse need to discuss and agree upon which rules to enforce and how that effort can best be realized. They then need to have a family meeting to share this information with the youngster. While the child might not like having to respond to these new rules, she will be learning self-discipline and self-control, traits very much needed in the world outside of one's home.

Agreeing on discipline styles is often not an easy task. We all come from different backgrounds. Our values and discipline approach come largely from the way we were raised. In addition, children absorbed values and discipline from both their biological parents. Now a stepparent is coming in with yet another group of ideas. How can the stepparent and parent work out the rules for this newly formed household?

1. Discuss together what the rules of the home have been thus far. Write them down. This is not a meaningless exercise. It will force you both to put vague thoughts into words.

2. Then rate which rules seem important to maintain and why. You may both decide that it isn't worth fighting about the kids making their beds each day as long as they keep the door shut. On the other hand, you may decide that bed making is a good habit to get into and that it fosters self-discipline and a sense of order. Whatever you decide, make it a unified decision and agree that it will be enforced.

3. Determine how well previous house rules have been enforced. Was this effective?

4. Prioritize the rules in the order each of you rank them. Then discuss your rankings, giving the reasons why you did so.

5. Compromise on points as needed so both rankings are similar. You may be surprised to realize that what you may have thought was inviolate really wasn't as important as you once believed.

6. Sit down with your children and stepchildren and go over the rules. Use whatever approach is appropriate for the youngsters' ages.

▪ DETERMINING WHO'S THE BOSS ▪

As with most things, even the experts can't agree on who's in charge when it comes to discipline. One school says the biological parent should be the one in authority. Another claims that the stepparent needs to become part of the team immediately and be supported by the biological parent. Probably something in between is preferable.

"My past experiences as a stepchild (both parents remarried) have helped me to understand the problem areas I could encounter with my stepson," Jody, mother of a stepson and two biological children said. "For example, punishments are dealt out by my husband. Being saddled with the stigma of being a stepmom, I didn't want to be the bad guy, too. This doesn't mean that transgressions against me by my stepson are not punished. They are simply reported to my husband for him to deal with. Fortunately, my husband backs me up ninety-five percent of the time. The remaining five percent are what cause friction between my husband and me. I didn't feel it was my place to start disciplining my stepson when my husband and I married. Alan was four years old when we met and his dad and I were married when Alan was eight years old."

Another stepmom, Lucille, told how she handled discipline problems with her fourteen-year-old stepdaughter, Suzanne. She also has a son who is seven, and she and her second husband are the parents of two-year-old twins.

"In handling Suzanne I always have to keep her mom, dad, and stepdad in mind. If I don't, I get in hot water with any or all of them. This fear (on my part), makes me step back further (and let her get away with more) than my other kids. Her bio dad is overly protective and tends to excuse her when he shouldn't, and her mom and stepdad can often get defensive and not want to hear the whole story. It has gotten much better with all her other parents, but I am still not one hundred percent clear to deal with her misbehavior on my own. She knows this."

While discipline is important to bring respect and order into a household, the stepparent probably should move slowly in enforcing discipline in the early days of the marriage, unless he or she also brings children into the blended family. In either case, the biological parent should take the lead with necessary disciplining, while at the same time letting the stepparent see what the rules are, how they're enforced, and what discipline has been effective in the past. He or she also needs to let the children know that if the biological parent is absent, the stepparent is charged with the total responsibility of enforcing the household rules and maintaining discipline. It's very important for children to look at the parenting team as just that, a team, with both adult members fully vested with authority.

According to Eric Q. Tridas, medical director of the Child Development Center of Tampa Children's Hospital at St. Joseph's, "Children and parents may be engaged in a family partnership, but the parents are the managing partners. They have the experience, capital, and the responsibility to take charge." Even if you're a stepparent who has never had children, you still have life experience. Think of becoming a stepparent as a battlefield promotion: Now you're a leader.

Most of my interviews with biological parents said they encouraged the stepparent spouse to become involved in discipline immediately, with the caveat that he or she deferred to the biological parent when the adults disagreed. "That creates a united front when the children are present. We can argue our case behind closed doors," one mother said wryly.

▪ SETTING UNDERSTOOD BOUNDARIES ▪

Most of us have no difficulty setting boundaries for our household pets. Ringo, the dog, is allowed on the couch, but not the bed. Ginger, the cat, is not permitted to sit on kitchen counters. Bingo, the bird, may not fly around out of his cage when Grandma's visiting. But when it comes to our kids, we tend to vacillate. We say the kids have to keep their rooms clean, but we don't define what we mean by clean. We say, "No TV until homework's done," but we let them join us in watching the Academy Awards or a football game. Our mealtime rules vary from "Eat one bite of everything" to "Just eat what you want," and then we wonder why we end up as short-order cooks or feel angry and resentful as we scrape the remnants of a gourmet meal into the garbage can.

Boundaries are not prison walls. They don't confine. Instead, they define actions, telling our kids what actions and behaviors are acceptable in our household. Remember, it's important to stress to our children that these rules apply to them in our home; the rules may be different at their other biological parent's home. One is neither right nor wrong, just the way it's done.

Despite what we may think, kids do want boundaries. Often I overheard one of my kids saying to a friend, "Oh, my mother won't let me do that." Sometimes it wasn't even something we had discussed, but it gave our children the security (and pride) in letting their friends know that we had set limits for them because we cared. Of course, as teenagers these boundaries were crossed from time to time, but they knew ahead of time what punishment was in store.

One of our teenage sons came home after curfew. I was sitting in the kitchen waiting for him. "You're late," I reminded him as he came in and was startled to see me sitting up. "You missed curfew."

"I'm not that late," he began. "Besides, I think it's crazy for boys to have curfews."

"In this house they do," I said calmly. "You agreed to the time we set. I'm afraid you won't be able to drive the car for a week."

With that he threw the keys at me and marched off to bed. After a week of enduring being driven to school by his sister, he came to me. "I've been thinking about it," he said. "I don't think there's anything wrong with a boy having a curfew." I agreed and handed him back his keys without so much as a lecture. Enough had been said . . . and learned.

Another of our sons came to his father and me with a problem. "My curfew is earlier than any of the younger girls I'm dating. It's embarrassing and makes it hard for me to even go to a movie and get home on time."

We had to admit that we had set an early curfew for our own convenience. He was one of the younger kids and we found it hard to stay up past 11:30 p.m. waiting for him to get home. But he was right. The older ones had enjoyed midnight curfews at his age. We agreed to change his curfew to a later time and he agreed to abide by that time. Boundaries are not carved in stone. They are more like the crossbar in the pole vault, able to be moved when the individual is ready.

▪ GIVING CHOICES ▪

Although adults must make major decisions in your home, it helps to give your children choices whenever possible, keeping in mind their age and maturity level. Whenever it's possible to include their input, offer a choice.

- Don't make it an open-ended question and keep the selection to a few choices or you'll never reach consensus. For example, don't ask, "What would you kids like to do over the Fourth of July?" Instead, narrow the options by saying, "Would you rather go to Aunt Jenny's for a picnic over the Fourth of July or to the fireworks and sailboat races at the lake?"

- Make it clear that the majority wins.

- Never offer choices you are not willing or able to carry out.

▪ BEING CONSISTENT ▪

Although it is difficult at first for children to experience different styles of discipline in each of their parents' homes, they soon get accustomed to it, rationalizing that "We do it this way at Daddy's and that way at Mommy's." What's really confusing and harmful to them is when there's no consistency within one home.

In his book, *Living in a Step-family Without Getting Stepped On*," Dr. Kevin Leman writes, ". . . the key to discipline is finding the right balance between giving the children plenty of *love* and giving them adequate *limits* that hold them accountable for their actions."[1] To this I add, it also helps to develop your own personal version of "the look" which lets them know when they're pushing the package.

My grown children surprised me by saying that they knew exactly when to toe the line as children, when to push no further.

---

[1] Dr. Kevin Leman, *Living in a Step-family Without Getting Stepped On*, (Nashville, 1994), 209, Thomas Nelson Publishers.

"It was when you gave 'the look,' " my daughter said. "It was a cross between a glare and a stare, but its message was clear: Enough is enough."

When you give in, "just this time," your kids will know exactly next time just how far to push before you weaken. But when the rules are firm and have been clearly explained and accepted by everyone, there is no reason to surrender, even if it means it truly hurts you more than the child.

▪ CRITICIZING BEHAVIOR, NOT THE CHILD ▪

Kids of a divorce, no matter how long ago it occurred, are still hurting and sensitive. When they've misbehaved, it's very important not to tell them that *they're* bad. Saying that they're "bad" just reinforces their feeling that they, in some unknown way, were bad and caused their parents to split up. The behavior may be bad, never the child.

It's okay to say, "I feel very disappointed when you act up in public," but not "You're a bad girl for acting up at the grocery store."

▪ LISTENING ▪

If you've read this book from the beginning, you'll remember that there was a section on listening in Chapter Three. Why is it repeated? Because many discipline problems are created because the parents didn't make the boundaries clear at the beginning or because the children weren't listening. In addition, because a stepparent comes into an already existing family, he or she may not know the family dialect. The biological parents may have often said, "No, for the last time," when it really wasn't the last time at all. The kids knew they could whine, fuss, and pout and eventually get their way. If you're a stepparent, listen to the verbal cues in your new family. If you feel they're in conflict with the desired behavior, privately discuss it with your spouse.

LISTEN TO YOUR SELF

There's a wonderful thought-provoking T-shirt advertised in many mail-order catalogues that reads, "Mirror, mirror, on the wall, I'm like my mother after all." It made me smile. Although I swore that I would never say some of the hurtful things my mother occasionally said to me in anger and frustration, I once heard myself saying to one of our kids, "I don't care what you do!"

I froze, because I immediately recalled my silent response as a child when my mother said that exact phrase to me. "Please do care. I want you to tell me that I can't do what I said I wanted to." As soon as I heard myself saying that same phrase, I asked my child's forgiveness. "I'm sorry I said that. I *do* care. I care very much what you do." And then I explained why whatever she was begging to do was off-limits.

LISTEN TO WHAT ISN'T BEING SAID

We need to listen attentively to what our kids are saying or asking instead of considering our response or prejudging their request. We also need to try to determine the unspoken message. When one of my sons was under ten, he and I talked about his asking for permission to visit a particular friend's house. I didn't feel comfortable about his going there. Both parents worked and my son's friend and two teenage brothers had the run of the house. I knew the older boys drank and suspected they used illegal drugs as well. As I listened, I gathered that my son wasn't too keen on going over to his friend's house at all. He just didn't want to be the one to say "no."

I asked if my conclusion was correct. He sheepishly admitted that it was. We talked about how we could handle the situation in the future so it wouldn't be awkward for him. We came up with the following game: If he asked for permission and didn't want to go, he would preface his request with "Mother." If it were something he wanted to do, he would say, "Mom," as was his customary name for me. It was my cue, when I heard him call me the more formal, "Mother," to say he couldn't because we had other plans or to give some other excuse. He was relieved because he didn't have to refuse his friend directly. As he grew older, he became more comfortable with saying, "No," but until he gained confidence, he appreciated our team solution.

POOR BEHAVIOR MAY BE A CRY FOR ATTENTION

Poor behavior can be caused by a fatigue factor, which can also be a cry for more attention. Getting accustomed to all the changes in a newly blended family can be stressful, especially on a young child. This added stress may affect sleeping habits, such as the child having more difficulty in falling asleep or staying asleep. Gaining a new stepsibling or half sibling who also shares the bedroom can affect sleeping habits too.

Sometimes a child just misbehaves because he or she needs more "hugging time." When our kids were little, we encouraged them to come and tell us whenever they felt they needed an extra hug. Even now that they're grown, they still occasionally ask for some hugging time, as I do when it's been a particularly tough day. (We're an equal opportunity family, especially when it comes to hugs.)

MISBEHAVING MAY BE A CRY FOR REASSURANCE

If you're listening in the fullest sense to words and actions, you may sense that a youngster needs some reassurance that he or she is still important. This may be especially true in a blended family when stepsiblings enter the scene and a child is displaced in the birth order, such as no longer being the baby of the family or the oldest. It also may arise when an "our baby" comes into the blended family, if the former baby feels displaced. The acting out you could easily put down to naughtiness may be no more than trying to redefine him or herself and adjusting to a new position in the blended family.

▪ PRAISING ▪

Augustus and Julius Hare, English Anglican clergymen of the late eighteenth and early to mid-nineteeth century, knew how to use praise to help with discipline. They wrote, "The praises of others may be of use in teaching us, not what we are, but what we ought to be."

Most of us want to please others, even if it's a stepparent whom we aren't sure we really like. Yet even young children sense when they're being falsely praised. Instead, focus on something—even if it's the only thing—the youngster has done properly and praise that. "I like the way you put all the blocks away," "I appreciate your calling to say you'd be late. That was very thoughtful," or "You set the table beautifully. Thank you for thinking of it," are just examples of praise even by omission. Don't spoil the effect by adding that the blocks were thrown into the toy box so it wouldn't close, the phone call came because you had given the child a personal telephone card, or the knife and spoon were on the wrong side.

Praising children raises their self-esteem. When they feel better about themselves, they are more likely to want to follow the rules. Be careful that you spread this honey around, however. If you neglect one of the children in the family, especially if it's one of your stepchildren, you may reinforce that youngster's feelings of unworthiness and he or she will live up to the perceived expectation you have set forth.

Be careful too about creating a scapegoat in your blended family, where one child is blamed for everything that goes wrong and becomes what author Vimala Pillari, D.S.W., calls "the burden bearer." Children who have become scapegoats in their families suffer from low self-esteem and a strong sense of guilt. If you sense that everyone (including the adults in your family) is constantly pointing fingers and blaming one person for every problem that arises, consider getting family therapy.

▪ PUNISHMENT ▪

Are you surprised to find a separate section on punishment? If so, it's because most of us think of discipline as punishment. But it isn't. Discipline is defined in the *Random House Dictionary of the English Language* as "training to act in accordance to rules." Punishment, on the other hand, is "a penalty inflicted for an offense or fault."

The purpose of discipline is to teach children self-control, responsibility, and a sense of right and wrong. It enables them to make decisions and to feel confident about those choices. It prepares them to exist in the world today and to lead happy and productive lives.

When we punish a child for an infraction of the rules, we need to be certain that we have been positive role models for those rules. Parents who encourage their children to lie about their ages in order to get a cheaper ticket for a movie or air fare are hypocritical when they punish those same children for lying about homework assignments or practicing music lessons. I stopped using spanking as a punishment when my children were small when I heard myself saying to one of them, "This will teach you not to hit your brother." It sounded ridiculous even to me. It must have been equally so to my relieved child as well. In the future, I found it far more effective to say, "We do not hit in this house. Go to your room until you can find a better way to solve your disagreements." And they did.

■ PUNISHMENT MAY DIFFER IN EACH PARENT'S HOUSE ■

When biological parents have joint custody, the children will quickly realize that just as the rules may differ from house to house, so does the punishment. One parent may use "time out" while the other believes in spankings. One may take away privileges such as television watching or playing on the computer while the other just lectures or yells. While it would be easier on the children if the biological parents could agree on the same punishment for infractions of rules, this compromise rarely seems to occur.

In some cases, when the biological parents communicate effectively, each will honor the other's punishment restrictions. "Your father said you aren't permitted to watch television for a week so you won't be able to here until that week is up," a mother tells her youngster. Others, however, argue that each household must enforce the punishment within those confines and not expect the other parent to require compliance in his or her house.

My personal feeling is that as rules differ from household to household, so does the punishment. One parent may call upon punishment for infractions that the other would overlook or consider minor. Unless the deed was truly one requiring a strict hand—such as creating bodily harm to self or another, use of alcohol or drugs, and so on, the punishment should be carried out in and restricted to the home in which the behavior was presented.

As with most decisions, however, the final action of this matter should really be determined by the two adults most responsible for the child's well-being, the biological parents.

▪ TEN RULES FOR MORE EFFECTIVE DISCIPLINE ▪

Children need discipline in their lives so they know what's expected of them. It is vital for them to have this structure for behavior to make them feel secure, loved, and a valuable part of their family. These ten rules may help you to become more effective in setting up rules for your blended family.

1. Explain the rules in a way that is age appropriate for each of the children.

2. Be consistent.

3. Lower your voice, which forces them to listen.

4. Never threaten what you can't/won't deliver.

5. Let the punishment fit the deed.

6. Don't name call.

7. Speak to the act, not the actor.

8. Teach cause and effect.

9. Let bygones be bygones.

10. Stay in the present.

CHAPTER SEVEN

School Issues

"There is no school equal to a decent home and no teachers equal to honest virtuous parents."

—MOHANDAS KARAMCHAND (MAHATMA) GANDHI

Nowhere in the above quotation do you find any suggestion that the "honest virtuous parents" cannot be divorced or that one of them cannot be a stepparent. That's because the quality of parenting is what's really the important issue. But it's vital for all parents, especially those who are going through a divorce or remarriage, to let the school know so the teachers, coaches, and administration can be watchful for any signals that the kids are having difficulty adjusting to the situation.

Although you obviously don't have to invite them to the wedding, your child's teachers and other school officials should be notified about your forthcoming nuptials as soon as your youngster is told. Your remarriage is bound to affect your child in some way. Unfortunately, it's often adversely. While your remarriage marks the beginning of your life with a new spouse, it also ends your child's dream that you and your ex might get back together again.

Susan Foster, principal at Gorrie Elementary School in Tampa, Florida, suggests that the marrying parent bring the soon-to-be stepparent to meet the school personnel, especially if he or she will be interacting in any way, such as helping with carpooling, working in the classroom, or acting as a chaperon for field trips. "This type of introduction makes the stepparent feel more of a part of the team and lets the school personnel know that he or she will be supportive of the child's best interests."

Other changes in family structure such as a new baby on the way, alternative custody arrangements, illness, or death of a grandparent or some other family member, may also affect the way a youngster adjusts to school. Don't minimize the effects of your child's traveling back and forth between the two parent's homes either. Many school officials believe it takes some children two to three days to readjust after visiting the other parent and as much as a month to get back in step after being with the other parent for the summer.

Be watchful for teachers who inadvertently create unnecessary problems in their desire to be helpful. In one preschool class, the teacher was trying to prepare her charges for the new babies that would come to a number of their homes that spring. "Your mommy and daddy won't have as much time for you when the new baby comes," she told the youngsters. Fortunately, she proudly related this discussion to one of the mothers (who was horrified). This mother informed the others, who then had to re-assure their children that although the new baby would take up some of their time, infants slept a great deal and there would be plenty of Mom-time to go around.

▪ MAKE MEETING THE TEACHERS AN ANNUAL EVENT ▪

Don't think that once you've met with your child's teachers and told them about your remarriage that you can sit back in the future and just wait for the regularly scheduled parent-teacher con-ferences. As children move up through the grades, they are as-signed to new teachers each year. Although your child's records probably mention your remarriage and the fact that there's a step-parent in the family and/or the fact that yours is a blended family, the new teacher may not notice it.

THE "TELL" OR "DON'T TELL" CONTROVERSY

There's a great deal of controversy on the "should you tell" issue. The biological parents and stepparents I interviewed were divided on what was the best way to handle this situation.

A stepmother said, "My stepson's biological mother is out of the area so her involvement is rare. On my stepson's school emergency information, I'm listed as the "Mother," since I'm close by and my husband likes things to appear "normal." His logic is, "Why tell someone we're a stepfamily unless they ask?"

I personally feel that the more information you can share with your child's teacher and the school administration, the better the flow of communication. This said, remember that you certainly don't need to go into the gory details of who did what to whom. Just offer as much as the teacher and other school officials need to know. When a teacher understands that there may be extra stress at home because of intense stepsibling rivalries or custody disagreements, he or she can pay closer attention to your youngster.

School performance is usually a good standard against which to judge how a child is coping with divorce and remarriage. If there's a sudden change in behavior or falling grades, the teacher can quickly alert the parents to avoid potential problems from developing. You may think that teachers should give this kind of careful scrutiny to everyone in the classroom. While that would be ideal, the reality is that when some classes have thirty or more students, it's often difficult to remain that observant.

Letting your child's teacher know that you have remarried and now go by a different surname prevents embarrassment, too. It allows the teacher to be more name sensitive, so he or she doesn't mistakenly address your child's stepfather by your child's last name. It also reminds the teacher and school administrators to rethink traditional school events that ignore the realities of multiple parents and grandparents that are unique to blended families. Increased sensitivity to the makeup of nontraditional families would prevent schools from scheduling activities such as a "father-daughter dance," Mother's Day and Father's Day parties, and other programs designed for the now endangered intact nuclear families with only one mother and one father.

PREPARE FOR THE NEW SCHOOL YEAR

The beginning of the new school year involves far more than just buying your kids new shoes and the "in" lunch box. It means meeting with your child's teacher and sharing whatever information you think will help the teacher get the most from your child. The education process has to be a team effort, with parents reinforcing what is done in the classroom and with teachers using what they have learned about each child to help youngsters grow socially and educationally. Bolstering self-esteem is a vital part of this process.

Make an appointment to talk to the teacher *before* the first day of class. There's usually a three- or four-day period before classes begin when teachers get their rooms ready for the incoming students. While it may seem easier to just wait to talk until you bring your kids to school that first day, it will be far less effective. Teachers are swamped on that first day, greeting their new students, trying to learn names, maintaining a semblance of discipline, while handing out forms and school supplies. It's not very conducive to personal chats with parents.

Be honest. If your child suffers from a feeling of intense rivalry with stepsiblings or with a recent "our baby" addition to the family, share that with the teacher. It may show up in his or her behavior in class and on the playground or playing field. If your youngster still feels insecure and anxious since your divorce and remarriage, share that too. Most schools have guidance counselors and/or social workers, professionals who are trained to talk with youngsters who are having difficulties in coping with some aspect of their lives. Sometimes an objective listener can ease the way a little. It also is helpful to most children to realize that they aren't the only ones faced with getting along with stepsiblings, a stepparent, a new home and/or school, and possibly, a new baby in the family. You're paying taxes for these services offered by your school system, so you might as well take advantage of them.

Realize too that you may be faced with a teacher or school administrator who is biased against divorce in general and stepparents in particular. He or she may be convinced that stepfamilies are "bad," or at least, "second rate." While you probably won't hear this philosophy stated in so many words, you may get subtle clues, such as "We only have time for each child to make one holiday gift for parents," or "Is his real father available to come for our Dad's Day program?"

Don't waste time trying to convince this dinosaur that it's time to update his or her thinking on the "broken home" mentality. Instead, show by your actions that your blended family is working together and is a happy and healthy one. Volunteer as a couple to help out at school activities, in the library, or on the special "community in the school" days. Let the teacher observe your child's stepparent as he or she demonstrates true caring and commitment to this child by marriage. If you and your ES can work together comfortably, illustrate that by example as well. Hopefully, your modeling of what blended families can be will help to transform the teacher's negativity into a more positive viewpoint. What you do tells so much more than what you try to say, especially to someone whose prejudice keeps him or her from listening. Think how much more pleasant you will have made it for next year's class of kids from blended families. There's bound to be some. Remember the statistics: Over 1,300 new stepfamilies are created every day.

▪ BE PREPARED ▪

By arming teachers, coaches, and school administration with an advance warning of changes in your child's family life, they'll be able to be on the lookout and be prepared for possible emotional upsets or acting out behaviors. Many schools have counseling groups for children in stepfamilies to meet with peers to discuss issues that bother them and to learn appropriate ways to handle their fear, guilt, resentment, and anger. But don't expect school personnel to be mind readers; educators can't help if they are not fully informed of changes in a family status.

COMMUNICATE EFFECTIVELY

Although Chapter Three deals with the importance of effective communication in all areas of blended family life, one of the most crucial situations involves that between parents and school personnel. If communication between parents and school personnel is a two-way street, both can reach their shared goal of giving each child a good education, says Judith Myers-Walls, Purdue University Extension specialist and associate professor of child development and family studies.

Obviously, logistics must be considered to facilitate this communication. Difficult at best when the biological parents are married to each other, effective communication often requires more planning when the parents are divorced and have remarried to partners who also may be involved with the child's upbringing.

PUT DIFFERENCES ASIDE

Some experts encourage teachers to hold two separate school conferences when parents are divorced to prevent disagreements and down-and-out fighting during this important meeting. Being the mother of a fourth grade teacher, however, I have more than a slight prejudice in this matter. Our teachers are tremendously overworked and underpaid. Asking them to conduct two conferences for every child with divorced parents could, in some classrooms, add as much as two to four extra hours of meetings. It says a great deal about the various individuals' commitment to a child's best interest when the teacher is willing to schedule two separate conferences, but the child's own biological parents won't agree to sit in the same room for fifteen to thirty minutes.

I offer the suggestion that school conferences and other school activities should be considered an event (like bar mitzvahs, confirmations, and weddings) for adults—who care and love their child—to act their age. Put aside your personal antagonisms and meet together with your child's teachers as "honest and virtuous parents," concerned parents who want only the best for their child. The one exception to this advice is when you need to notify the teacher or school counselor of a problem that can not be discussed in front of your ES. Negative issues affecting the children, such as your ES's drinking habits, his or her refusal to put the kids to bed on time so they are exhausted when they're at school, or your ES's lack of responsibility which makes your kids tardy frequently, should be pointed out in a separate conference. The purpose of this meeting should not be to depict how horrible your ES is, but rather to inform the school personnel of the situation so they can work out ways to help your kids without your involvement in these matters.

SETTING UP A MEETING WITH TEACHERS AND OTHER
SCHOOL PERSONNEL

With everyone's busy schedule, it's often difficult to arrange a meeting time that is satisfactory to everyone involved. But it's important to make the effort to arrange it. Don't add to your ES's possible anger or hostility by scheduling a time that you know isn't convenient to him or her.

Points to consider when setting up appointment with school officials include:

- Learn when the teacher/administrator is available for a meeting.

- Discover the best time of day for the parents to meet.

- Ask if it is best to call the teacher at home or school to set up the appointment.

- Determine whether you prefer the teacher to call the parents at work or at home.

- Discuss whether parents and teachers consider notes preferable to phone calls.

A good time to get the answers to some of these points is at the beginning of each school year, before any issues have arisen. Then, when you do need to arrange a meeting, you have prepared the groundwork. "Be sensitive to when the teacher or school official has time to meet," Myers-Walls says. "You don't want to be seen as a distraction; you won't get quality interaction."

Other teachers warn, "Don't become a chronic complainer. By

all means, speak up if you see something at the school that displeases or concerns you. It's all right to discuss things and make suggestions, but not to demand or threaten us. Consider the priorities and don't fuss about the little things. If you make a commotion about everything or bring in an adversarial attitude, you'll no longer be taken seriously. What's worse, your reputation will precede you and your child. We teachers do talk in the faculty lunchroom, you know."

Remember that we—teachers and parents alike—all respond better to positive strokes. If possible, contact the school personnel first with something you're pleased about or that seems to be working well in the classroom, before you hit them with the problem.

WORK OUT PINCH POINTS WITH YOUR EX-SPOUSE BEFORE THEY AFFECT THE CHILD

Ideally, it would be nice if you and your ex could work out problems *before* they arise. As that obviously isn't always possible, do settle them quickly before they fester, causing both parents to become frustrated and angry, and your child embarrassed. While the problems may differ from person to person, the tug-of-war responses usually are the same.

Say, for example, that you receive a note from the school guidance counselor saying that your child (for whom you have shared custody with your ex), has expressed an interest in joining the school's "stepchildren peer support group." You think it's great and sign the form giving your permission and send it back. But your ex (who may or may not have received the same note), doesn't think it's such a hot idea because he hasn't trusted therapists in any form since the two of you went for marriage counseling and he swore the woman therapist sided with you all the time. He forbids your child to go to the sessions.

You're furious with him. You feel as though you've lost face with the guidance counselor. He's furious with you and doesn't trust the guidance counselor who "didn't even have the courtesy to write to me directly." Your child is embarrassed because you two never agreed on anything before the divorce and still don't; and the guidance counselor wonders why she just didn't go work for UPS, where she could make more money and have less aggravation.

How could this situation have been prevented? Through pre-planning and proper effective communication:

1. Both parents should inform the school before the year begins that they *each* are to receive any letters, forms, invitations, newsletters, report cards, or other materials being sent from anyone at school. In addition, the school should be sure that when there is joint custody, the names and addresses of both parents are listed in the school directory.

2. Either parent receiving such information should call the other, describing what it pertained to and discuss what actions need to be taken.

3. The parents need to confer, either by phone, e-mail, or in person, to discuss the pros and cons of the particular decision.

4. The parents must agree that the decision will be based on the needs of their child and not be used as a power struggle to prove one or the other "right."

5. In the previous scenario, the parents probably would need additional information from the guidance counselor to learn what actually occurred in these sessions and what the goals were. This knowledge might have raised the father's comfort level enough so that he would have permitted his youngster to take part in the peer group meetings.

The same courtesy, communication, and compromise can be used to work out most school situations such as who acts as chaperon on school field trips, how to arrange carpooling during rehearsals for the school play, and whether your child should take Spanish or Latin. Always ask your child if he or she has a preference. Even young ones may have strong opinions. (My father insisted on Spanish against my mother's preference for Latin. He won. But as a writer, I've always regretted not having a background in Latin. No one ever asked me which language *I* wanted to take.)

■ KNOW YOUR SCHOOL'S LEGAL REQUIREMENTS ■

Almost every local school board has set up legal requirements for schools concerning situations that may arise on site with children of divorced parents, especially when the relationship between the two biological parents is hostile. To save you and your child embarrassment, learn what the rules are in your district. Although the following may differ in some degree depending on your state and the particular school system, this list is fairly typical:

RELEASE OF CHILD

Teachers will only release a child to the person who has enrolled that youngster in the school, unless there is a local court order to the contrary. If there is some problem that is unusual in that situation, the administrator should advise the parent who does not have custody to apply to the court if he/she wants the child released. The only situation in which a child should be released to a parent, other than the parent who registered the child, would be in a situation where there is a *recent order* from a local court giving custody to the parent who wants the child.

VISITATION AT SCHOOL

Does a parent who does not have custody have the right to see a child at school? Normally, the school system is not a place for visitation. In an emergency situation, of course, a divorced parent could see his or her child at the school site, but only if there are some pressing circumstances for such a visit. The divorce courts usually provide for visitation with children, and the courts generally would not want this visitation to occur on a school site. Further, it has long been the policy of school boards not to allow various schools to become involved in domestic disputes.

AUTHORIZATION AND PARENT PERMISSION

Many school boards now accept authorizations and parent permission forms for such things as medical treatment, field trips, and so on, from either parent, regardless of who has physical "custody," as long as the Final Judgment of Dissolution of Marriage reflects that the parents have "Shared Parental Responsibility."

IS "SHARED PARENTAL RESPONSIBILITY" THE SAME AS "JOINT CUSTODY?"

No. "Shared Parental Responsibility" means that both divorced parents share in decisions concerning the child's education, religion, and health care needs. The final decision will be from the custodial parent.

"Joint Custody" means that the child is in residence with each parent part of the time.

EMERGENCY CONTACT

The principal may contact the parent who does not have custody of a child in the event that the parent who has custody can not be located in cases of emergency. However, every attempt should be made to contact one of the natural parents of the child.

RELEASE OF INFORMATION

A parent who doesn't have custody, but requests copies of report cards and/or other information concerning the child should be provided the information, if possible. However, the child's home address and telephone number should not be released without the permission of the custodial parent.

WHAT RIGHTS DO STEPPARENTS HAVE?

A stepparent living with the natural parent who enrolled the child in school is entitled, unless otherwise instructed by the natural parent, to obtain information about the student who is living in the same household.

▪ OFFER STABILITY WITH FLEXIBILITY ▪

This isn't a conflicting statement. You *can* do both. In fact, you must. Stability without flexibility is rigidity. That's not healthy for people or even buildings. Architects figure in a sway tolerance in buildings so the structures can move slightly in high winds. If they were perfectly rigid, they would snap. And offering flexibility without any semblance of stability is confusing and distracting for most of us, and especially so for youngsters in a blended family.

Although you and your ex may have painfully worked out an agreement for joint custody, remember that a child's work is school. The activities—programs, sporting events, plays, and social events—are important for your child's growth and social development. Don't insist on having "your" night alone with your child if that means that your son or daughter will miss final rehearsal or practice before the big event. Be willing to trade days if your ex needs extra time to help your youngster complete a science project or find the perfect dress for the prom. It may not seem as important to you, but it is to your child.

▪ DO NOT EMBARRASS YOUR CHILD ▪

Your child's school is his or her workplace. Peer opinion and respect is as important to kids as it is to us. Never, never embarrass your kids at school by picking a fight (verbal or physical) with your ES or with his or her new mate. It not only diminishes you in your kid's eyes, but it also is poor role modeling for the other kids in the class.

Be mature and polite to your ES and his or her new spouse, even if you have to keep biting your tongue and your cheeks ache from the effort it takes to smile. You can't? Then change your thinking pattern.

▪ CHANGE THE WAY YOU THINK ▪

You have within you the power to change the way you think about things. You've probably used that ability to alter other behaviors, such as losing weight, quitting smoking, beginning and adhering to an exercise program, and so on. The main reason you did those things was that **you wanted to change your behavior**.

You also can change your emotional response and the negative behavior you display toward your child's other biological parent in front of your youngster and his or her classmates. Focus on your love for your child, not how much you dislike your ES or his or her new marital partner. Visualize yourself being civil and at ease when you're at school assemblies, plays, or sporting events and your ES is there with his or her spouse. Focus on their good points, such as how supportive and kind the stepparent has been toward your kid, and how responsible your ES has been toward the kids you had together or, at least, how much your children really love your ex.

When you begin to think more positively about them, you'll begin to act and react that way. You'll shudder when you hear horror stories about other divorced parents who choose to be absent from their children's plays, sporting events, and honor assemblies because the school auditorium isn't big enough for the two of them. You'll shake your head when you see former married couples who come to school events, but act in such a way that is hurtful, embarrassing, and traumatic to their children—children that they both claim to love. You'll find you actually feel better when you begin to banish bitterness and negative thinking from your mind. Your kids will notice and thank you, even if they can't bring themselves to verbalize it.

Youngsters in blended families have a lot more stress to deal with than kids whose biological parents are still married to one another. Practice positive thinking. Don't become one additional source of stress for your kids.

Remember what Shakespeare wrote in *Hamlet*. "There is nothing either good or bad, but thinking makes it so."

▪ CREATE A UNITED FRONT ▪

Put up a united front and attend as many of your child's school functions as you can, even if you know your ES and his or her spouse will be there. Kids can use all the emotional support they can get. When your youngster sees that he or she has a *four*-parent cheering section, you'll find that you've done much more than just putting on a "happy face." You will have helped to raise your child's self-esteem. What better gift is there for parents to give a child they all love?

CHAPTER EIGHT

Customs and Rituals

"The forces pulling on families are just too strong in the modern world. Ultimately, we must decide either to steer or to go where the river takes us. The key to successful steering is to be intentional about our family rituals."[1]

—WILLIAM J. DOHERTY, PH.D.
Author and marriage and family therapist

From the beginning of human civilization, every group, no matter how big or how small has created its own customs and rituals that give rise to their definition for acceptable behavior. These customs and rituals deal with everything deemed important to that society, including worship, food gathering and preparation, values, manners, and the celebration of life cycle events. There are vast differences in customs and rituals between countries, so much so that most governments have protocol officers who must be aware of even subtle nuances in order to prevent their leaders from making embarrassing faux pas through ignorance of another country's customs or rituals.

There also are differences in customs and rituals between varying economic levels, religious organizations, social groups, and most certainly, between families. While the customs and rituals of a biological family develop slowly over the years, stepfamilies are often suddenly faced with diametrically opposed traditions. Sometimes these differences can be easily negotiated and compromises worked out. At other times, however, especially when both partners bring children into the remarriage, conflicting customs and rituals come together as with a sonic boom, creating a tremendous amount of negative fallout.

---

[1]William Doherty, *The Intentional Family: How to Build Ties in a Modern World* (New York, 1997), pp. 10, Addison-Wesley.

▪ WHAT ARE RITUALS? ▪

According to William J. Doherty, Ph.D., a practicing therapist and Director of the Marriage and Family Therapy Program at the University of Minnesota, there are three important aspects of a ritual:

1. The activity must have meaning or significance.

2. The activity must be repeated.

3. The activity must be coordinated.[2] (pp.10-11)

▪ WHY CUSTOMS AND RITUALS ARE IMPORTANT ▪

Over time, most families create their unique form of customs and rituals that suit their lifestyle. These traditions become the way things are done in that particular home, the way holidays and life cycle events are celebrated, mealtime and bedtime routines are carried out, and privacy is observed. They define what is expected and give order to lives. Children in that environment grow up knowing that these are the "rules," the boundaries that are followed. Although the actual customs and rituals may seemingly have no actual importance in themselves, the fact that everyone in the family understands what they are and chooses to observe them gives them their significance.

The knowledge that the rituals are unchanging offers a sense of comfort and security to the entire family. It deepens their sense of belonging. In a world where nothing else seems too permanent, these rituals often serve as a lifesaving device, keeping a family afloat.

But when a couple is divorced, these rituals necessarily may change or die off altogether. A single parent may feel depressed, especially at holiday time and not feel much like cooking the usual traditional Thanksgiving feast, dyeing Easter eggs, or decorating the house for Christmas or lighting the Hanukkah candles. Birth-

---

[2]Ibid., pp. 10–11.

day celebrations may lose some of their sparkle, and even everyday rituals such as bedtime stories, celebration dinners, or rainy day Monopoly or Candyland tournaments may fall by the wayside. New rituals must be created to fill the void in order to make this new family comprising a single parent and children feel comfort in being a unit once again.

When that single parent remarries, however, certain of these former rituals with which the children have finally grown comfortable, may be altered or omitted altogether as no longer being useful in fulfilling a need. The family, composed of the once-single parent and the children has widened to include a stepparent and possibly, his or her children. This new ingredient to the family pot also mixes in their customs and rituals to spice up (and possibly overwhelm) the household. Some of these new rituals may seem strange or unfamiliar or be in direct conflict with the ones observed by the former family unit. Children may be reluctant to let go of the established rituals that made them feel secure after the parent's divorce and may resent this newcomer who has different ideas about the "right" way to decorate a Christmas tree, celebrate a birthday, or spend a vacation.

Never underestimate the importance of your family's rituals and customs. They are ingrained in our earliest memories and, like the proverbial old shoe, feel most comfortable to us. While a blended family must eventually compromise and create its own unique customs and rituals, don't be too quick to throw out the old. Many youngsters in blended families are much more willing to give up their rooms to a new stepsibling than to forgo their familiar rituals. Move slowly.

▪ COMPROMISING WHEN CUSTOMS COLLIDE ▪

When a couple first marries, it's often difficult for them to merge the customs and rituals they bring from their respective families. It can become a common source of conflict, creating arguments and hurt feelings. Perhaps one spouse comes from a home where a great deal was made over birthdays and anniversaries. The other partner comes from a home where little attention was paid to these events. Understandably, the first person may feel forgotten and neglected when his or her birthday passes with little, if any, observance.

"My first husband made a big deal out of my birthday," a thirty-year-old woman recalled. "He had the kids sing a little song for me and there were special silly little presents hidden all over the house. When I remarried, I expected the same type of celebration. But my new husband had never celebrated his birthday with much fuss, let alone anyone else's. For my first birthday with him, he didn't take the kids to buy a gift or get a card for me. And there was no card or gift from him either. I felt very disappointed.

"Luckily, he's a communicator. He urged me to talk about my feelings and was shocked when I told him that I felt let down and unappreciated. I guess I expected him to be a mind reader. My birthdays since that first forgotten one have all been fun, for me, for him, and for the kids. I don't feel the celebration is diminished in any way because I had to tell him what I liked. It's like sex. If you don't tell, it doesn't jell. Now he's even beginning to enjoy celebrating his own birthday. But we don't play mind-reading games anymore. It's been a good lesson for all of us."

It's very much the same problem when kids become part of a blended family carrying the experience of specific customs and familiar rituals that give them comfort and a sense of security from their biological family. When the unknowing stepparent ignores "the way we've always done it," resentment may flourish. While the stepsibings and stepparent promote theirs as the only "right way," the other side argues for their way of doing things. Communication is vital to work out compromises that are satisfactory and comforting to all involved.

Compromise is especially important when religious backgrounds are blended, especially when handling emotionally-charged events such as first communion, bar or bas mitzvahs, and weddings. Surprisingly, it is often the grandparents, not the parents, who create the most conflict.

"I knew what I was getting into when I married a Catholic widow with three children," a Jewish man told me. "While she knew I had no intention of converting to Catholicism, she also knew I was supportive of her raising her kids in the Catholic faith and that I agreed to raise any children we might have as Catholics as well. The trouble began when my father said he wouldn't come to our wedding, even though I had found a rabbi to co-officiate with the priest. My mother talked him into coming, but there was an obvious strain at the wedding.

"That was nothing, however, like the fuss he made when our own child was about to take her first communion. Once again, Dad put his foot down. He said he couldn't bear to watch his own flesh and blood taking communion. He announced he wouldn't come, and this time he couldn't be budged. My wife was understandably distraught and I felt torn. I had been raised to honor my parents. But I loved my wife and had made a commitment to her. I was angry with him for ruining what should have been a beautiful day for my family.

"After it was over, I met with my father and told him that I loved and honored him, but that my new family had established its own traditions that were important to us. I stressed that I personally wasn't abandoning Judaism, but that I had to be loyal to my wife and children who were Catholics. He seemed to understand and admitted that he was sorry he had missed what was a special time for me and for my wife. He really liked her and loved all of our kids. That week he made a point of apologizing to her and said it was difficult to compromise at his age, but that he understood the need for it. Communication was the key. I wished I had talked man to man to him before the wedding."

• HOW TO BLEND YOURS, MINE AND OUR •
CUSTOMS AND RITUALS

Most of us grow up with the firm belief that the way our family had of celebrating a holiday or special event is the only way to do so. It takes a great deal of adjustment, even when we're adults, to accept that perhaps it's okay to have pecan pie, not pumpkin for Thanksgiving and to open Christmas presents on Christmas Eve, not the following morning. Usually, however, newly married couples make the necessary compromises and have both pumpkin and pecan pie, and open one gift on Christmas Eve and the others that next morning.

When kids are involved in blended families, however, it gets tougher because each tradition comes with a symbolic price tag marked, "Pre-divorce." To change how things were done when Mom and Dad were still married seems disloyal to kids, stirring up many old feelings that have not been resolved. There is often a profound sense of loss of what was familiar and comfortable to them. According to Dr. James Bray, a psychologist at Baylor College of Medicine in Houston, "Many stepchildren are still upset over their parent's divorce and have not adjusted to their new family." He offers the following suggestions to help resettle the nest in time for the holidays:

- Hold a family planning meeting (See Chapter 3). Assign duties among children, and be sure the older children are included.
- Consider alternating holiday visits from year to year.
- Create new family traditions. Rituals then become shared experiences that can help solidify a blended family.

Recreating customs and rituals for a stepfamily sounds a lot easier than it actually is. It requires effort and enthusiasm and is a great deal like making a patchwork quilt. You take a piece from here, another from there, and bind them together with patience and love until they unite, forming something unique and most special.

DON'T TRY TO ACCOMMODATE EVERYONE'S FORMER RITUALS AND TRADITIONS

When you merge two families, it's tempting to try to accommodate everyone's former traditions and by doing so, become too overloaded with special customs and rituals. To be sure you aren't dragging along some no one really cares about, ask both sets of kids to prioritize their favorites. For some, it may be the special blue plate the birthday child gets to eat dinner on. For others, it may be making cookies in the shapes of dreidels and stars the Sunday before Hanukkah or pasting up the paper chain on Thanksgiving night, so they can break one ring off each day until Christmas arrives. It may be as minor as getting bagels and cream cheese before you all read the Sunday paper or as major as a trip each summer to one of the national parks and marking it on the family map.

WEED OUT TRADITIONS THAT NO LONGER SATISFY

Don't try to guess which traditions are most meaningful to your children. You're bound to be surprised. Our family used to celebrate a child's birthday with cake for breakfast. It made the entire day begin with a special celebration and made the birthday boy or girl feel singled out from the time he or she got up in the morning.

Once the kids got older and became more concerned with weight and health issues, I suggested dropping the cake for breakfast tradition. You should have heard the outcry. My suggestion was unceremoniously vetoed.

On the other hand, when many of their Christmas "stocking stuffers" became more expensive than some of the wrapped gifts, I timidly asked how they felt about retiring the stockings my mother had made for each of them when they were born. To my surprise, the kids all agreed that they could buy their own toothbrushes and razor blades, and would rather have the smaller gifts like jewelry, pens, or audiotapes wrapped as gifts. So before you stop any tradition, ask the kids how they feel about it.

■ CREATING NEW CUSTOMS AND RITUALS ■

Families often identify themselves by the memories of customs and rituals, so never minimize the importance of these events. To merge them when a stepfamily is formed takes caring, communication, and compromise.

- She serves her children dinner in the formal dining room, on her good china and with the good silver. He and his kids eat take-out chicken from a bucket or Chinese food from cardboard cartons in front of the television. Compromise? Have one night a week that's a dress-up dinner and another that's a picnic in front of the TV.

For dress-up dinner, encourage the kids to dress nicely. Set the table with flowers or candles. Use the occasion to subtly teach manners. Show the boys how to pull the chairs out for their sisters (and mother or stepmother). Boost the kids' self-confidence when they go out with others by helping them learn which fork or spoon to use in the privacy of their own home. If you're not sure yourself, check in an illustrative cookbook or a book on manners. Use cloth napkins. We have napkin rings with each person's name engraved, but department stores and specialty shops have fun ones in the shapes of animals, shells, flowers, and so on.

For the picnic night, throw a blanket on the floor and use paper plates. Fix or bring in typical picnic foods like fried chicken, hot dogs and hamburgers, deviled eggs, potato salad, and cookies. Make the dinner casual and fun. Afterwards, play a game of "Go Fish" or word games.

With either meal, you're doing more than feeding your family. You're cooking up memories.

- He reads three books to his kids every night before putting them to bed. She lets her kids fall asleep in front of the TV. What to do?

A good compromise would be encouraging reading aloud on school nights and letting one night on the weekend be a "slumber party," when the kids could stay up late. There needs to be a pre-agreed upon curfew time, however, so the parents can get some sleep and the kids don't get overtired. Many families, who began by reading bedtime stories to their kids, have continued the custom of reading aloud as the children have grown. These families take turns reading aloud to one another for half an hour after dinner from the classics or from the Bible. It's a wonderful alternative to watching television.

. Christmas is a major production for her and her kids, with a tree, decorations she's had since her own childhood, and a special night set aside for decorating the house. Everyone gets a lot of gifts—including some with silly tags from famous people. He and his kids celebrate Hanukkah and receive one gift a night. How can they compromise on what many call "The December Dilemma?"

"By some estimates," according to an article by Jerry Adler in the December 15, 1997, issue of *Newsweek*, "one in three American Jews lives in an interfaith household . . . The comparable figure for Catholics, according to a 1990 survey cited by psychologist Joel Crohn, an authority on mixed marriages, is twenty-one percent percent; for Mormons, thirty percent, and for Muslims, forty percent."[3] The Jewish/Christian couples I interviewed all said they incorporated both traditions in their blended homes, lighting the Hanukkah candles and playing with dreidels, as well as trimming a tree and hanging stockings for Santa Claus or "Hanukkah Harry," as one person called it. Many Jewish/Christian stepfamilies also hold a Passover seder in their homes, with both sides of the family joining in to celebrate this historic celebration of freedom.

These rituals draw families closer together and give their members a sense of identification, even if the ritual doesn't represent one's own particular religion. It doesn't have to be something major, either. One of the best Christmas Eves I ever experienced was one at which our five children organized and presented my husband and me with a private concert of Christmas carols. The fact that they had secretly planned and rehearsed it together was one of my favorite gifts ever.

[3]Adler, Jerry, "A Matter of Faith," *Newsweek*, December 15, 1997, p. 50.

He and his kids spend vacations camping out in the woods, sleeping in tents, catching fish and cooking them over a campfire. She and her kids spend their vacations in America's major cities, going to zoos, museums, and seeing stage plays.

Even this family can work out compromises to create new traditions for their blended family. While it would seem simplest to just continue with each group spending their vacation doing what they enjoy—and many blended families did just that—the family would be drawn closer together if each group occasionally tried something new that the other liked. The campers could join the cultural set to sample a taste of the city, perhaps going to aquariums and zoos and other nature attractions. The theatergoers could try their hand at a dude ranch, a one-day fishing expedition, line dancing, or a picnic and a campfire. The old commercial that said, "Try it, you'll like it," might be true in this case. In any case, sampling what the other members of the family enjoy will open new vistas and give history to a blended family in need of creating memories. Even if both groups decide they really hate the other's favorite pastime, they will have shared in the experience and have greater insights concerning the various activities. Perhaps with this newly found cohesiveness, the entire blended family can seek out additional activities to do as a family.

▪ BE OPEN TO NON-HOLIDAY RITUALS ▪

Be open to creating non-holiday rituals too, such as non-birthday parties, a Fourth of August celebration (for the month with no holidays in it), or a special dinner for the night before school begins. Look for opportunities to create special rituals like going to a movie together after Thanksgiving dinner, family vacations, annual family garage sales with the money going to a specially selected charity, or Sunday night family dinner.

Pay special attention to celebrating rites of passage such as graduations from elementary school, junior high, high school, and college. Plan a trip alone with just the high school graduate and the parents. Let the new Eagle Scout or Gold Award recipient select his or her favorite restaurant for the entire family to go to celebrate after the ceremony. Have a party to celebrate great report cards. Just remember to spread the honors around. If three of your kids make the honor roll, also celebrate the fourth one's beating his or her personal best on the swim team.

MEALTIME IS A RITUAL

Mealtime is an important ritual for a family because food always involves a great deal of emotion. Our family always ate most of our dinners in the formal dining room. The table was set with a cloth, napkins, personalized napkin rings at each designated seat, my best china, and silver flatwear. Often we had candles. Although my own mother had saved her china and silver for company, I preferred my mother-in-law's philosophy that family was just as, if not more, important than company. The kids' behavior seemed to imply that they appreciated the effort.

The mealtime rules were few, but were strictly adhered to. Shirts were required (but shoes weren't). Lively discussions were permitted, but no arguments or name calling. And, since this was a time before the universal acceptance of telephone answering machines, the youngest one at the table had to answer the telephone, although messages were taken unless it was an emergency.

Frequently, the kids asked to be excused right after they had finished eating. But as they grew older, we all often lingered at the table, enjoying each other's company and conversation. To this day, we still have regular Sunday night dinners together, with as many coming as are able. It gives us a wonderful opportunity to touch base with family members and take a refreshing time-out with those we love. Our family has grown, enlarging the circle as our children marry and both grandchildren and step-grandchildren enter our lives. Although I've often heard our adult children tell their friends about our dinner hours, I had never really considered them our family ritual until I began writing this book.

Another favorite mealtime ritual is one that my husband and I have combined with his brother and sister-in-law. It began when our kids were small. It now has grown to include her ten grandchildren and my two. We call it the Shimberg–Shimberg Holiday Party. It alternates each year between my house and hers. Held every December 23, it's our way to get our kids and their kids together, now including grandchildren too, for the holiday season and to enjoy a meal and fun together. As we both have some children who have intermarried, it is neither a Christmas nor Hanukkah celebration, but rather a ritual that pays tribute to the love of family, the continuation of the generations, and highlights interaction between not only the adult first cousins, but also the younger second cousins.

THINK SMALL

Like mealtime rituals, your blended family rituals need not be major ones. What's important is their predictability and enjoyment for the entire family. Consider just a few suggestions to get you started:

- Berry picking at a farm on the first Saturday of July or August, and then making muffins out of what's left after the nibbling.

- A Family Olympic Day with croquet, checkers, kick ball, and tug-of-war. Everyone should win a ribbon. The object is fun, not competition.

- An annual garage sale with the proceeds going to the family's favorite charity.

- A Fourth of August picnic with family colors selected to replace the standard red, white, and blue familiar with the Fourth of July.

- A St. Patrick's Day party.

- Volunteering as a family to help serve food at a homeless shelter, paint a house for an elderly person, or deliver food for Meals on Wheels.

· Canoe or go tubing down a local scenic river on the first day of spring. (Be sure to have life jackets for everyone.)

· Renting a cabin in the woods or at a lake each year.

Schedule your family days at a time all the kids will be with you. Otherwise, those who are with their other parent will feel left out. Family days are a good way to build memories while you're having fun. Don't expect every experience to be ideal, but often the ones that fall flat are the ones everyone laughs about throughout the years.

SOME RITUALS CAN BE ONE-ON-ONE

All rituals don't have to have a total family focus. They can be parent-child or stepparent-stepchild oriented. A stepmother, who was having trouble communicating with her teenage stepdaughter, made a reservation for two at a nearby health spa. After a day of exercising together, massage, having facials, manicures, and pedicures, the two came home laughing and kidding one another. They may have lost only a pound or two, but they gained much more. That was five years ago. Now close friends, they still schedule an annual get-together at the spa.

Stepfathers also enjoy creating one-on-one rituals with their new stepchildren, such as opening day at the ballpark, an annual trip to see a college or professional football game, or an overnight hunting or fishing trip. On these occasions, a deep closeness can develop without the presence of another adult or the other children. We all like (and need) personal attention. I can still remember an all-day fishing trip spent with my father when I was no more than eight or nine years old. While I still think fondly of that event, I can't recall whether or not we actually caught any fish. What didn't get away, however, were the memories.

Bedtime rituals create special moments too. It's more than just reading a book or two with your child or stepchild. It's the one-on-one that says, "I really care about you." It's a time when confidences may develop and trust builds, opening communication that otherwise seem locked behind emotional doors. Tuck-in routines such as saying prayers together, singing a bedtime song, or just kisses on the forehead, nose, and mouth help the children in your life drift off to sleep feeling loved, cared for, and secure.

▪ BE SPONTANEOUS ▪

These special non-holiday traditions are especially important if you share your kids with your ES. Be spontaneous. If your kids will miss their blended family's traditional tree trimming festivities because it's their other parent's turn to have them for Christmas, put the tree up for Thanksgiving. Make taffy and have an old-fashioned taffy pull after the kids' exams, before they go to their other parent's house for the summer. Go on a nature walk to honor the first day of spring and see the buds on the trees. Listen for the kids to say, "This is fun. Let's do it again." That's your tip to consider making that activity a special part of your new family's history.

▪ FAMILY MEETINGS ▪

Family meetings are one of the most important rituals for a blended family (or any family, for that matter). Don't put off organizing this vital tradition. It not only draws your family closer together, but it also keeps communication lines open and makes each member of the blended family feel special.

See Chapter Three for suggestions on how to organize and conduct family meetings.

▪ OPEN YOUR HEART AND MIND ▪
TO MAKING MEMORIES

The opportunities are there to create new customs and rituals that will bind your new family together and create precious memories. Open your heart and mind. Be willing to be creative. Listen to your kids for their ideas, and most important, make the time to make memories. It's worth it, for your sake, your family's sake, and for the future.

CHAPTER NINE

Follow the Money

*"It's good to have money and the things that money can buy, but it's good, too,
to check up once in a while and make sure that you haven't lost the things that
money can't buy."*

—GEORGE HORACE LORIMER,
Editor, *Saturday Evening Post*, 1899–1936

*M*ost of us are fascinated by money. There's little doubt of it. Whether we have too much or too little, there's a hypnotic quality innate in its lure. Reference books overflow with quotations concerning money. Money or the lack of it has been the subject of hundreds of books, movies, and television shows. Recent examples include the best-selling nonfiction book *The Millionaire Next Door* by Thomas J. Stanley and William D. Danko and television shows *Lifestyles of the Rich and Famous* and *The Millionaire*. Millions of people spend money on lottery tickets, roulette wheels, poker, and even Bingo cards, hoping to win more money. Yet it all comes down to an old Yiddish Proverb that says, "He who'll pay has the say." This maxim has great meaning for those couples who are creating blended families.

▪ MAKE SENSE OUT OF THE EMOTIONS OF CURRENCY ▪

Financial issues are one of the most emotionally loaded subjects that stepfamilies must learn to handle. In this era of "tell all," most people will openly discuss numerous topics that formerly were considered taboo—including sexual matters, physical and mental health problems, addictions, and personal stories of domestic violence, even to a nationwide television audience. But try to open a discussion that focuses on their finances and they clam up.

Despite that, our daily conversation is replete with references about money. We speak of wanting to (or needing to) win the lottery. We tell our kids, "Rich or poor, it's nice to have money," and remind teenage sons, "It's just as easy to love a rich girl as a poor one." But when it comes to talking about our finances on a more personal level, we grow mute. The "e" in "money" must stand for "emotion" or "evade."

Unfortunately, there's no avoiding it. The highly charged emotional issues revolving around money need to be addressed in stepfamilies, however painful they may be. (Interestingly, the Spanish word for pain, "dolar," sounds something like the English word for "dollar.") Left dangling, rather than realistically being faced, money disputes can tear at the very fabric of a marriage relationship.

Financial concerns quickly multiply in a stepfamily, not only because it costs more to fund two separate households (or three or more, depending on the number of former marriages and children the individuals may be supporting), but also because there are so many people involved. A stepparent may be partially supporting his or her children by a former marriage in addition to helping to foot some of the bills for stepchildren in the present marriage. Those children's noncustodial biological parent may be sending money to help pay for the children's expenses in the custodial household, while at the same time, supporting his or her own stepchildren as well as children born to the present marriage. One or more of the parents in the mix may also be spending money to help care for an elderly parent or a chronically ill sibling. Add to that mix monies that may come (or be withheld) courtesy of various sets of grandparents and you can see how complicated the issue becomes.

▪ MONEY IS POWER ▪

Money also carries with it symbolic power and control. Whoever holds the checkbook carries the clout. Remember that in your financial dealings with all your present and past family members. If you can separate your thinking from the symbolic interpretation of money and focus on what it is needed for—the well-being of your children—your financial negotiations should go more smoothly.

In many ways, the financial aspects of a blended family become more difficult because each adult formerly was running his or her own household as a single parent or individual and made all the financial decisions independently. Although some families headed by a single parent are funded to some degree by grandparents, most of them get by on the single wage earner's income plus child support from the noncustodial parent.

Nevertheless, as the only adult in the home, decisions concerning money could be made quickly and sometimes rather capriciously. There was no need to go into a joint conference to decide whether or not to buy a new car or a big screen television set, take a vacation, or switch jobs. Once used to this type of autonomy, it's often very difficult to remember that you're now a member of the financial committee and not just the treasurer.

It's especially difficult for women who were kept out of money management decisions during their first marriage and now have become capable money managers to feel totally comfortable in letting go of the purse strings and agreeing to share them with their new spouse.

"I'll admit it was difficult in the beginning of my remarriage," said a forty-year-old lawyer and mother of two teenagers. "I'd buy a new chair for the living room and be surprised when my new husband said he felt left out of the decision. At first I thought he was being overly sensitive. The more we talked, however, the more I realized that I had been a single parent for so long, I forgot what it was like to be a team player. My advice? Remember that even the quarterback has to tell the play to the rest of the team if they're going to be successful. Marriage is a team sport. Discuss major purchases with your spouse before buying them."

• OUR ATTITUDES TOWARD MONEY ARE "INHERITED" • FROM OUR PARENTS

Most of us bring into adulthood a value attached to money that we learned in childhood. It may have been imparted by over-hearing whispered conversations about potential cutbacks, layoffs, and poor investments. We may have been admonished that "We can't afford it," when we asked for something.

On the other hand, we may have learned that "Money's only good for spending," or "If it costs more, it's got to be better." One parent may have been tight with money, while the other secretly handed out extra to the kids, with the whispered warning, "Don't tell your father (or mother)." Security and, in many cases, love itself was expressed to us as children in the emotionally laden five-letter word: money.

OUR ATTITUDE WITH MONEY MAY BE IN CONFLICT WITH THAT OF OUR SPOUSE

This symbolic meaning to money is deeply ingrained and may be in conflict with those of our marital partner. For example, if one of our parents was addicted to gambling so that we never could count on school tuition money or even rent money being available when due, we may have the tendency to squirrel it away for the proverbial rainy day. If our father was keeper of the treasury and doled out an allowance to our mother and to us in a de-meaning way, we may have resolved to have our "own" money kept separate from the joint household funds.

In our former marriage, we may have been the keeper of the coin and payer of all bills. When a new spouse wants to know the cost of various household expenses and wants a monthly account-ing of the checkbook, "Don't you trust me?" pops into our head. You may have agreed with your ES about putting as little down as possible on your house and carrying a heavy mortgage. It may be a shock to learn that your new spouse doesn't believe in mort-gages. These and other viewpoints toward money can erupt into violent confrontations with a new spouse when we create a step-family.

Disagreements also can arise with an ES over how money should be spent. The ES may have worked his or her way through college and believes that his or her kids can do the same thing when it's their turn to go. You may think that it's all right for them to work for their expenses, but that it's the parent's responsibility to pay for tuition.

Meanwhile, in the background, but still there, is your new spouse murmuring that getting through college today is hard enough without having to worry about money. He or she is willing to help defray some of the costs if you and your ES will do your part. Then another player is heard from. It's your ES's spouse. He or she thinks the kids should pay for a quarter of the college expenses so they'll have a vested interest in doing their best work. Chances are various grandparents will give you the benefit of their advice too, especially if they have money earmarked for their grandchildren's education.

You certainly won't be short on suggestions. But before a compromise can be reached, all of you will have to distill the real issue—should the kids pay for part, none, or all of the expense of going to college—with the emotional baggage that surrounds it.

THERE'S NO "RIGHT" OR "WRONG" ATTITUDE TOWARD MONEY

People show a great diversity in their attitudes toward money. Some individuals believe in paying cash for everything. "If we don't have the money, we don't get it," is their creed. Others go by the "If God didn't want us to charge things, He wouldn't have invented credit cards," philosophy. There's no "right" or "wrong" feeling toward money, just yours. But it's important to share your emotional response to money with your spouse so he or she knows where you're coming from to prevent surprises and ugly scenes. If your partner believes money is to be spent and "there's plenty more where that came from," you'd better admit it if you have fear of losing everything and need a comfortable amount in savings in order to feel secure.

ON WHOSE ACCOUNT?

Who pays for what is a major issue in most stepfamilies. The majority of the couples I interviewed said they pooled their money into a joint account. A few kept a separate account for the money received by the ES that was to be used for the children's school tuition, summer camp, special lessons, and medical needs not covered by insurance. When there is shared custody of the children, each parent usually pays for "living expenses" while the kids are with him or her. They then share major expenses such as school tuition, fees for sports and lessons, and so on.

> "My ex-wife has never been a very good money manager," said a father of a six-year-old girl. "So I just pay for all of our daughter's expenses."
>
> "It just shows how really smart she is about money," the man's new wife said bitterly. "She doesn't have to spend any of her own money on her kid." She later added that she and her new husband might not be able to afford to have any children of their own because of his attitude toward money.

Nevertheless who pays for what and who writes the checks is an issue that should have been resolved before you remarried. If it hasn't, now's the time.

One of the easiest ways to decide this issue without emotion is to give it to the person best suited for the paperwork involved. When we were first married, I happily volunteered for the job. Unfortunately, at that time I didn't have a separate bill box so bills were always getting stuck into my reference books as bookmarks or caught in the pages of a manuscript, where they'd remain until it was time to do the next rewrite on the book in progress. When

my husband finally discovered that I was reconciling the checkbook by rounding numbers off to the nearest dollar, he replaced
me as bill payer, much to my relief, I might add. But if I had felt
diminished or a loss of power by being "fired," it might have triggered anything from an argument to an all out war.

MAKING ALLOWANCES

There is great variety of how parents give money to their children and there was little agreement among my interviewees as to
which way was preferable. Although few parents or stepparents
begrudge buying kids clothes, paying for school tuition, fees for
Little League or gymnastics, the issue of handing over spending
money is far from cut and dry. Here is just a sampling of some of
the various methods used for giving money to the kids:

- A set allowance given regularly with nothing required of the
  children.

- A set allowance given regularly, but with specific chores required in return.

- Spending money given to the children according to the various household chores they've performed.

- Spending money given to the children when it's requested.

- Spending money given to the children when it's requested
  only if the parents agreed it was needed.

- Spending money given as a clothes allowance.

- No spending money given to children if they are old enough
  to earn it themselves.

One of the problems in blended families concerning money for
the children arises when the stepparent strongly disagrees with the
amount and the way the kids' money was distributed in the original biological family. It's also tricky if your way of giving money
to your kids (as well as the amount) differs greatly from the way

the stepparent gives it to his or her kids. If this is the case in your blended family, work out a compromise as a couple, so you can be in total agreement before presenting the new plan to the kids.

Also try to work out a compromise with your ES over the kids' spending money so you know whose responsibility it is to hand out allowances. Open and honest communication also prevents your giving an agreed upon amount of money to the kids each week while the cash flows freely at their other parent's house. Sometimes this can work against the more generous parent as the youngsters may feel guilty getting so much from one parent while the other is unable or unwilling to match it.

Another difficulty that arises in blended families is when grandparents give large cash gifts to their biological grandchildren, but nothing or a mere pittance to their step-grandchildren. Although older youngsters may seem to understand, it still can create intense sibling rivalries. Try to encourage the grandparents to give smaller cash gifts to all the children and put the larger amounts into a college fund or trust fund for their biological grandchildren, if they so choose.

As everyone is entitled to his or her own bias concerning children's spending money, I am sharing mine. I personally encourage parents to give children a regular pre-agreed upon allowance on a weekly basis. It should not, however, be tied into chores. Family members shouldn't get paid for regular chores; they do them because they are part of the family. Money can be given, however, for selected one-time jobs such as cleaning out the attic, repairing the doghouse, painting porch furniture, and other age appropriate tasks. But the children's allowance, what Grace W. Weinstein called their "practice session," in her book, *Children and Money: A Parents' Guide*, should be theirs to spend—however foolishly or wisely as they so choose. How can they learn how to handle money if they don't have any to handle?

Our children drew up a budget for their allowance every September before school started. They had to figure out how much they needed for entertainment (movies, tapes, and magazines, but not books. We always were willing to pay for their books), makeup and "fun" toiletries, charity at religious school, snacks, and so on.

As they grew older, of course, the costs of dating, gas for the car, and more "have to have" clothing appeared on the budget.

Then they presented us with the budget and had to defend it. (We had a line option veto long before the President of the United States did.) Often the kids didn't get the amount they requested. At times, they got even more because they had underestimated costs of things. After all, the purpose of the allowance was to give them independence, to teach them something about money management, and to make them more realistic concerning the cost of things. It also taught them how to prioritize their wants and how to save.

DO YOU SHARE SIMILAR VIEWS REGARDING CHARITY?

This is another aspect of handling money that can trigger disagreement in all marriages, but may be accented in a stepfamily because of expectations from either or both the childhood home and the first marriage. Your partner may want to tithe, to give ten percent of your joint income to charity, whereas you may prefer giving far less, feeling that you need every penny you can muster for yourself, your spouse, and the kids. Or you may want to give small amounts to a number of worthy charities, while your new spouse prefers giving one or two more major gifts to favored charities. Talk out your feelings regarding giving to charity, using the techniques described in Chapter Three.

If you and your spouse have difficulty in reaching a compromise, consider that starting a new stepfamily together might be a good time to begin new traditions of giving. Include the children, if they're old enough, and create family activities such as garage sales with the proceeds going to a charity everyone agrees on, working to build or repair a home for Habitat for Humanity, or work together at a shelter serving food to the homeless. There's far more to teaching the value of charity than just giving money. The gift of yourselves and your time may be the perfect way to help draw members of your blended family closer together. As American psychoanalyst Erich Fromm said, "Not he who has much is rich, but he who gives much."

• CHECK EMOTIONS FROM CHILD SUPPORT •

Never underestimate the emotional baggage attached to child support. Whether you're giving it or receiving it, emotion flows with the ink on the check. Money denotes power. If you're on the receiving end, you may feel demeaned and resentful if the check is late or, in your eyes, is too little. If you're the one writing the check, you (or your new spouse) may feel as though you're giving too much. Resist the opportunity for a power play such as withholding the check so your ES has to ask for it or not sending the proper amount so that he or she needs to call. Remember that child support goes to help support your child, just as you would have done if the marriage had not broken up. Review the amount periodically, to adjust, if need be, if extra costs such as braces, medical expenses, or special lessons arise.

If you're on the receiving end of child support, be honest and spend the money as it is intended—on your children. If your income increases, be willing to pay your fair share, as you would have if the marriage were still intact. Child support is about your kids, not about how you may feel about your ES. Never withhold your child's opportunity to see his or her other parent because the child support is delinquent. It's vindictive and will punish your youngster unfairly.

Don't keep your new spouse in the dark if your ES is inconsistent about sending the agreed upon child support check on time or often doesn't send it at all. You and your new mate both need that information for budgeting purposes.

In many cases, stepparents also contribute a great deal financially to their stepchildren's care, although their spouses may fret that it really isn't their responsibility. Those who do it do it for a number of reasons. It may be that the ES isn't consistent about sending child support checks, the amount the ES can afford to send doesn't cover the necessary costs, or the stepparent feels a commitment toward the spouse's children and just wants to help out. If it makes you uncomfortable to have your spouse helping to financially support your kids, discuss it openly. Never let it fester and develop into a major problem between you.

"I couldn't stand the way my wife's ex-husband patronizingly parceled money out to her for the care of their children," Anthony, a new stepfather confessed. "It reminded me of the way my mother had to plead for money for us kids, with my dad demanding that she account for every penny. I'd rather pay for my stepkids' expenses myself, which is crazy, since their dad makes so much more than I do. It's an emotional reaction, I know, but his stinginess drives me crazy."

▪ DON'T USE YOUR KID AS A BANKER ▪

Many divorced couples who still harbor bitterness and ill feelings toward one another, make their kids the courier or a pseudo-banker, forcing the children to ask their other parent for an advance on the child support, demanding payment, or requesting a loan. Don't do it.

Never put your children in the middle between you and your ex-spouse, carrying messages from one side to another. It's hurtful to them and gives them too much power.

Money issues, even those concerning your children, are adult issues to be discussed out of the children's earshot. Don't discuss these matters over the phone with your ES when your kids are home or when he or she comes to get the children with the kids hanging over the banister, trying to eavesdrop. Find a neutral spot. Kids should not be burdened with their parent's disagreements over money matters, especially when it comes to finances that are needed for them. Many of the adult stepchildren I talked with mentioned hearing their parents fighting over money matters—or their parent and stepparent fighting over money matters—as their major cause of distress growing up.

"In retrospect, it probably wasn't all bad," a twenty-nine-year-old man said. "My parent's fighting over money matters motivated me to work my way through college so I wouldn't have to ask anyone for money. As a kid, I used to hide in the closet so I wouldn't hear my stepfather complaining that my dad's child support check was late or not big enough to cover my expenses. I felt guilty every time I needed money for a field trip or new clothes. I earned a scholarship for a state school and worked at the dorm for room and board and spending money. That way, I was independent of them all. I didn't have to hear my dad's excuses about how he couldn't give me more because he had a new family to support. And it kept me from hearing my stepfather's tirade that he had already spent a great deal on me growing up and I wasn't even his own kid. I guess it did affect our personal relationship somewhat though," he added quietly.

▪ WHO PAYS FOR WHAT ▪

Deciding who pays for what is a task that would challenge Solomon himself. Certainly the courts have difficulty in making those determinations. That's why it really is best if the biological parents can work out the details themselves.

FLEXIBILITY

Even after child support is formulated, however, it can't be carved in stone. Situations change, undoing what you (and probably highly paid attorneys) spent so many hours working out. Certainly your remarriage, whether it's to someone with children or without, changes things. So does a child's chronic illness, a job change by one of the biological parents or the stepparent, grandparents needing more care as they age or become infirm, and a child being born into your blended family.

Do your children a favor by remaining flexible and realistic and being willing to revisit the child support plan on a regular basis. Agree between yourself and your ES that either of you may call for such a meeting when it's needed, that you'll meet at a time convenient to both of you, and that you'll both listen to what the other has to say, without prejudgment. In most cases, it's probably better if the only individuals at that meeting are you and your ES. Keep the new spouses out of the picture unless there's a very good reason for including them.

COMPROMISE

Be willing to compromise when you don't feel you can accept the proposed total financial package. This time you may give a little, the next time your former spouse may do the compromising. Try to keep emotion out of your discussion and stick to the facts. If you can't reach an agreement, bring in an objective party who can help mediate.

REMEMBER THE KIDS

The bottom line should always be that it's the kids who are important, not the money. Too many parents get caught up in the minutia of who pays for what and forget who gets the benefit— their children. Work out your differences like adults. If one of you gets a raise, wins the lottery, or becomes the beneficiary of an inheritance, be willing to negotiate with your ES for the benefit of your kids. Perhaps horseback riding or ballet lessons don't seem too vital to you, but they may to your child. Certainly orthodontics work, speech therapy, summer school enrichment programs, and other bonuses can make an important difference in your child's life. Forget the dollars and make sense.

■ RIDE THE MONEY TRAIN ■

When all is said and done, the money train rides on a circular track. It goes round and round and stops with what you and your ES can do financially for your children. Like the train tracks, you, your ES, and your children are linked together as long as you live. When you pull together, your children benefit, not only by being more secure financially, but also by knowing that, despite being divorced, their parents can still work together for their children's well-being. It's a tremendous comfort to kids who still love both of their biological parents.

Often, however, the train has two engines, with each pulling in the opposite direction. If you and your ES can't discuss money matters without fighting or rehashing how money problems affected and ruined your marriage, sit down with an objective person such as a qualified financial advisor, counselor, banker, or family therapist. It's really a fairly simple process once you get emotions out of the way as much as possible. You both have a finite amount of money. You both also have your own living expenses and one or both of you have a new family. There may be additional babies born into these new families. How can you both best spend what you can afford to help your children and still have enough for your new families? It probably won't be a static figure, but one that will shift back and forth like the tide. Illness in one of your families may make money tight for a while, one of you may be a victim of cutbacks at your place of business, or a roof may need replacing. Communicate promptly and effectively. Pull together. Your kids should be the beneficiaries of your money, not the lawyers you have to call in because you two can't agree.

▪ MAKE SHORT WORK OF LONG DISTANCE ▪

When you're the custodial parent, you can quickly spend a great deal of nonbudgeted money when your child has to use long distance to call his or her noncustodial parent. While you don't want to (and shouldn't) ban phone calls, you need to get the costs under control. What can you do?

"I sat down with my two kids, twelve and fifteen, and told them while I encouraged them to call their dad whenever they wanted to, phone bills were really getting out of hand," said a mother of two adolescents. "I treated them like adults and they responded as such. They came up with a set of rules they felt were fair. The rules included:

1. Setting a kitchen timer for a fifteen-minute limit. After that time, they were responsible for paying the bill.

2. They would try to call during "cheap" times, other than for emergencies.

3. They would write letters more often.

4. They would use e-mail, providing the computer usage time didn't get out of hand as well.

Their stepfather surprised them at Christmas with their own telephone and line, along with a $25-a-month gift certificate. The kids would be responsible for anything over that. It not only solved the long-distance dilemma, but it also drew them closer to their stepdad as they realized that he not only accepted their close relationship with their biological father, but actually encouraged it.

You also can give the kids telephone cards that they can use without money to call their other parent from a phone booth. You can buy these cards, good for varying amounts, at drug stores, grocery stores, convenience stores, and many other places.

▪ DISREGARD EQUALITY ▪

When I hear parents say, "I treat all my kids the same," I know something's wrong. Either they do and they shouldn't, or they don't, and they should be honest about not doing so. It's okay, you know.

NEEDS DIFFER

Children's needs differ and these needs may change from time
to time. One youngster may need his or her teeth straightened,
another may need speech therapy, and another may have a low
self-esteem and just need more hugs and encouragement. You
can't figure on setting an equal amount of money for each child.
It's more important to be fair than equal.

If your teenager needs a bike to get to school, you certainly
don't have to spend the same amount on your ten-year-old. Perhaps the younger child only "needs" some new educational computer games. Give to the need and share the love.

In some cases, your stepchildren's grandparents may have
agreed to pay for their college education. That could mean that
while your stepchildren will be able to go to any public or private
university they can get into, your own kids will have to try for
scholarship money, earn money for college, and use whatever you
can save for their education. Equal? No, and possibly not altogether
fair. But it is a realistic scenario.

Kids keep score of what their siblings (and stepsiblings) get
and measure it against what they don't have. It's a fact in all families, not just stepfamilies. You can help fend off the expected resentment by keeping communication lines open. "Yes, It's true
that you don't have to share a room with your stepbrother at your
dad's house and you've got your own television set and stereo
there. Here you don't. But your friend Mark has his own car and
you don't have one either here or at your dad's. And your buddy
John doesn't have a car or a stereo or a television set. What's more,
he shares his room with his twin stepbrothers who are eight years
younger than he is. We take a family vacation each year and like
spending our money for the fun times we have then. Every home
is different."

The theme, "Every home is different," is safe because it's a
nonemotional response and it states the fact. You may get a few,
"I'd rather be in Dad's home" or "I wish I lived with Mark," but

ignore those. In their hearts, your kids know they're loved, even though in their minds they feel they're being deprived.

> A mother of six (two "hers," two "his," and two "theirs") said, "I tell them to just handle it. Suffering's good for their souls. When I don't get uptight over their complaining, they feel it isn't such a big deal and go on to something else. Don't give them control over your feelings. Not ever."

▪ CREATE TIME FOR MONEY TALKS ▪

As with any other type of communication, you need to make time to discuss financial issues. See Chapters Three and Four on ways to best communicate with your ES. A few former couples find that it works best for them to sit down with the stepparents as well, so that everyone is completely aware of what the financial demands and needs are. Others prefer to deal with just each other, preferably at a neutral place where they can focus on the financial issues at hand. Whenever possible, try to keep lawyers out of your discussions. The money you'll have to pay for their services could be going to your children.

A parent and stepparent also need to discuss issues that affect them both. Throughout my interviews, I heard many fears and much anger expressed by stepparents pertaining to potential money problems and their rippling effects.

> "He said he wanted more children," a stepmother in her mid-thirties with no kids of her own said bitterly. "He knew I did. But then he lost his job when the company down-sized. His ex refused to take less in child support. The money that we were supposed to use to have our own child ended up paying for private school tuition for his three kids. Do you blame me for being bitter?"

"I don't mind helping to pay for part of my stepchildren's college," a stepfather admitted, "but I do worry how I'm going to pay for the kids we've had together. I don't think I can get my wife's ex to help me with mine, do you?"

"My husband and I struggle financially while my stepdaughter's mother and stepfather (who are extremely wealthy and have nannies, maids, an enormous house, and so on) can well afford to feed and clothe her," said a woman from the deep South. "I have a real problem with our paying total child support on a child when there's *fifty-fifty* custody. He didn't even want the divorce. Yet he pays for child support that isn't needed and we cover all her medical and dental. But we don't get to claim her as a dependent on our taxes. My stepdaughter says her mom takes our checks and goes shopping.

"I try not to get bitter over this, but it hurts when I can't get things for our little ones."

This woman's decision to try not to get bitter is a good one to follow. Becoming angry or bitter about monetary issues solves nothing and creates more stress and unhappiness in your life. Instead, try to keep the lines of communication open. Your mother's (or grandmother's) advice about getting more flies with honey than vinegar certainly applies here, especially if you equate your ES with a type of insect.

Under no circumstances should you involve your children in issues pertaining to child support. It's a no-win situation. You'll make them feel guilty for costing you money, angry that you're complaining about their other parent not paying what is owed, and confused about what really is an adult issue, not a child's.

DEFUSING FINANCIAL FIGHTS

Don't waste your time or energy fighting over financial issues. Use the communication skills you learned in Chapter Three. Stay to the point, which is finances for your children, not whether one of you is taking a three-week vacation in Europe, building a bigger house with a swimming pool and spa, or has a spouse who wears designer clothes. Keep the conversation as objective as possible. To help you stick to the issues at hand, write down an agenda and don't waver from it.

BRAINSTORM WITH CREATIVITY

Sometimes, when you sit down with your ES to discuss finances, you both realize that there really isn't enough money between you both to do all the things you'd like to for your children of the former marriage as well as those of your present ones. Try to discuss it like adults, respecting your joint concern for your children. When you banish emotion from these discussions, you often can come up with creative solutions.

"Despite our personal differences, my ES and I tell one another of major purchases we're making for our daughter, like her big Christmas gift or birthday present. It helps you to be prepared for the 'I have such-and-such at my Daddy's house' routine. It also eliminates the surprise factor so you can defuse the emotions that sometimes are attached to news of the other parent's gift.

"For older kids, I'd suggest thinking in terms of a mobile gift whenever possible, like a laptop computer that could be carried from house to house, rather than duplicating the computer at both houses. By communicating about gift giving, we've eliminated some of the one-upmanship games we used to have."

"My ex-wife and I agreed that we were spending a fortune on child care for our twin boys, age four. Although we both have good jobs, we felt we could be spending the money on the boys more satisfactorily. I casually mentioned that since my new wife was an at-home mom with our infant daughter, maybe she could look after them until whichever parent's turn it was to have them came home from work. At first she thought I was kidding. But the more we talked about it, it became the perfect solution. We asked my wife and she was delighted to have the boys. It's not only been good for the kids, but it also has created a friendship between my ex-wife, her husband, my wife and me. Our friends think we're crazy, but it works for us."

And that's what it's all about. Whatever works for you and the good of your kids is the way to go. It takes maturity and a little biting your tongue so the same things that made you end your marriage don't still make you go crazy. But you're in charge of that, you know. You can react negatively as you did in the past, or work in a positive manner, using self-talk to remind yourself that you're working together, "For the good of the kids."

MAINTAIN OPEN COMMUNICATION

Open communication is a skill needed by all the adults in children's lives. It allows you to speak up when the pinch points arise before they get out of hand. Open communication teaches you to listen, without judging or waiting to interrupt. And strong communication skills help you to renegotiate when necessary and improvise when the occasion demands it. Many of the scenarios described to me by those in blended families were unique and sometimes, even baffling to comprehend. But the important point to remember is that they worked for the individuals who had created them. And that, in the final analysis, is the vital issue.

There are many books available to families concerning money management. Two of the most complete ones are *The Wall Street Journal Lifetime Guide to Money: Everything You Need to Know* about *Managing Your Finances for Every Stage of Life*, edited by C. Frederic Wiegold and *The Lifetime Book of Management* by Grace W. Weinstein.

Money management is one of the most important issues in all of our lives. Granted, it becomes more intertwined and somewhat confusing when there are divorced parents with children, and emerging blended families, often involving additional children born into that blended family. Although few of us were taught fiscal management during our many years of formal schooling, money handling skills can be learned. So much of dealing with money matters in families is like dealing with life itself: listening to the needs of the other person, being creative and willing to compromise, and keeping your priorities straight.

CHAPTER TEN

Dividing the Children

". . . And the king said, Bring me a sword.
And they brought a sword before the king.
And the king said, Divide the living child in two,
and give half to the one, and half to the other.
Then spoke the woman whose the living child was unto the king,
for her affection toward her son was kindled,
and she said, O my lord, give her the living child, and in no wise slay it.
But the other said, Let it be neither mine nor thine, but *divide it.*
Then the king answered and said,
Give her the living child, and in no wise slay it:
she is the mother thereof.

—KINGS I, CHAPTER 3, VERSES 24–27

One of the most difficult concerns of divorce when children are involved is how to divide the children between their parents. The courts have struggled with this issue over the years, evolving from an almost unilateral decision to always giving custody to the mother unless she was obviously unfit in some way, to today's kinder and gentler resolution, which is usually some form of joint or shared custody. The majority of state laws today now have a presumption for or an option for joint custody unless it isn't in the child's best interest. But even when the judgment calls for one parent to have sole custody, the final result is usually the same: The children of divorced parents spend some time moving like chess figures from one square to another.

It really doesn't matter if the kids are transported cross-country or across the street or if you're on the sending team or the receiving team. You've got to have a game plan to make it a win-win situation for all involved. If not, these tumbleweed kids, who blow back and forth from one home to another, begin to feel that they have no real roots, and that they really don't belong anywhere. This can quickly lead to lowered self-esteem.

"I've always felt like a visitor in both homes," a fourteen-year-old boy confided to me. "My folks have joint custody so I spend alternating weeks in each home. At my dad's, I have to share a bedroom with my five-year-old half brother who's a real pest. He gets into all my things. I really don't have any privacy. My mom married a widower with eight-year-old twin girls, so at that house I'm expected to baby-sit constantly. I don't get along with my stepfather, so I just hang out with friends whenever I can. I can't wait until I graduate and go off to college."

■ IS JOINT CUSTODY "BEST?" AND IF SO, ■ BEST FOR WHOM?

Despite this longing for permanent roots, most experts claim that joint custody for children of divorce is the best solution possible for everyone involved.

SOLE CUSTODY

With sole custody, one parent becomes the "loser." He or she loses legal rights to the children, but often still has to pay for part or all of their support. While the noncustodial parent is usually granted "visitation rights," the visitations often are stilted and satisfying to none of the parties involved. Parents without custody often succumb to the "Santa Syndrome," buying the kids mountains of gifts and hauling them to Disney World, plays, or sporting events, sometimes all on the same day. There is little continuity between parent and child and the relationship suffers as does that of the grandparents, who also are deprived of consistent interaction with the child.

Sole custody also places a tremendous burden on the parent with custody. He or she (it usually is the mother), has no one to help with child care and no time off from its responsibilities. Finances often are strained because the custodial parent may not be able to upgrade skills to get a better paying job. What's more, the custodial parent is placed in an adversarial position with the ES, being required to determine when the noncustodial parent may or may not see the child.

JOINT CUSTODY

With joint or shared custody, parents are equal in their parenting responsibilities and have equal access to their children. Ideally, there should be more cooperation and less of a power struggle between the parents because each shares the children equally. There is the expectation that there should be no conflicts demanding that the kids choose sides. Grandparents and other members of the extended family also benefit from this arrangement. But the biggest winners seem to be the kids, who have the security of knowing that both of their biological parents love and want to care for them and that they see each of their parents frequently.

Joint custody requires the parents to work together for the good of their children. It demands cooperation and compromise, even if those were unknown entities during the marriage.

▪ WHEN ONE PARENT LIVES OUT OF TOWN ▪

Regardless if there is joint or sole custody of the children, their switch between households can create guilt and anxiety for an ES who lives in another town and must make the most of the child's "visits," which often seem too long and too short at the same time. It can create scheduling problems and anxiety for the spouse with custody and frustration, guilt, and uncertainty for the youngster who does the traveling. Yet with it all comes a certain modicum of benefit.

▪ WHEN YOUR CHILD GOES TO SEE YOUR EX-SPOUSE ▪

Despite your youngster's age, there's bound to be some uncertainty about going to see a parent after a long absence. Questions are normal, even if they're not verbalized:

- "Does my dad/mom really want me to come?"
- "Where will I stay?"
- "Will the other kids be nice to me?"
- "What if I want to come home earlier?"
- "Will I be missed at home?"

With younger children, there is a disruption of normal routine that, even with favorite sleep toys in tow and a favorite bedtime book, can not be alleviated. For older children, there is the sense of missing out on what goes on at home. Either way, there are tremendous pulls on these youngsters that we, as adults, must understand and not add to with our own emotional strains at this time.

▪ MAKE THE DEPARTURE EASIER ON YOUR CHILD ▪

While you may have nothing nice to say or think about your ES, remember that although you are divorced, your child isn't. Do your part by making the departure less traumatic for your youngster.

- Don't send messages for your youngster to communicate to your ex.

- Don't criticize your ex's housekeeping, choice of new spouse, or stepchildren.

- Don't mention all the great plans you have for everyone else while your youngster is gone.

- Don't carry on about how lonely you'll be.

▪ AVOID CUTTING THE KIDS IN HALF ▪

Although you and your ES are dividing the kids, you can keep from cutting them in half emotionally. However you divide them—your house one week, your ES's house the next or so many days here and so many there—let them feel that you and their other parent are united in wanting their best interests met. Don't play tug-of-war with your kids.

IF YOU CAN'T SAY SOMETHING NICE...

You put the kids in a terrible bind when you criticize their other parent or stepparent to them. Even if they agree with you, they're going to feel disloyal by saying so. What do you really gain by saying that their stepparent keeps a sloppy house or dresses like a bum? Think about what you might lose. Remember what Thumper's mother told him in the movie *Bambi*. It was: "If you can't say something nice, don't say anything at all."

DON'T ASK QUESTIONS ABOUT THE OTHER HOUSEHOLD

This is another way to hurt your kids. Don't ask them to describe what your ES's house looks like, what new furniture they may have bought, or to share any other "secrets" from the other home. Just ask if they had a good time and leave it at that. If they offer more details, such as "We went out to dinner to Fred's Fantastic Steak House," put a handkerchief in your mouth if you have to, but stifle the comment, "Well, your dad must be doing all right if he can take you all to that expensive a place. I wish we could afford it." You'll only succeed in ruining what had been a pleasant memory for your kids, but also make them resolve to never tell you anything else.

VOW TO WORK TOGETHER

Make a vow today that you will do everything in your power to work with your ES to keep your parenting relationship healthy, even as your divorce has forced you to divide custody for your children. It can be done. Most of the parents interviewed for this book have done so. Keep a positive outlook and look for the good in your ES. There must have been some for you to have gotten married in the first place. Focus on what works and strengthen it for your children's sake.

CHAPTER ELEVEN

Myths and Misses
(and what to do about them)

"A myth is like gossip; the more you repeat it, the more believable it becomes."

—ELAINE FANTLE SHIMBERG

According to *Webster's Ninth New Collegiate Dictionary*, a myth is "a popular belief or tradition that has grown up around something or someone." Myths are not new to our culture. They have been around since the beginning of civilization, explaining the "why" of something that people otherwise couldn't understand. They are found in the history of ancient Greece, Egypt, Ireland, Africa, and the American Indian, just to mention a few. Emile Durkheim, a French sociologist in the late 1800s and early 1900s, believed that "by examining a society's myths, a sociologist can discover its social institutions and values."[1] Therefore, myths can reveal just how individuals in a particular society think and behave.

In today's society, literature and the modern media probably are primarily responsible for the myriad of myths that have persisted in hanging over stepfamilies and in particular, stepmothers, like heavy storm clouds. Few of these myths make stepfamilies sound like an institution you'd like to enter. Here are just a few you may have heard or experienced yourself:

▪ MYTH: ALL STEPPARENTS ARE WICKED ▪

Shakespeare's brooding Hamlet was warned by his father's ghost that he had been murdered by (who else) Hamlet's stepfather (who also happened to be his uncle). Cinderella almost was

---

[1] *The World Book Encyclopedia*, (Chicago, 1973), Vol. 13, pp. 829, Field Enterprises Educational Corporation.

a no-show at the handsome prince's ball because her stepmother insisted she clean her room—along with the rest of the house. Other wicked stepparents included David Copperfield's stepfather, Hansel and Gretel's stepmother, Snow White's stepmother, and the list goes on and on.

As you can quickly see, you have been pinned with the stigma of being a "wicked" one even before you have entered into the stepparent fraternity or sorority. As such, you are not considered innocent until proven guilty. The burden of proof is on you.

How can you defend yourself against a history of wickedness? Some of those who have been successful in doing so suggest going on the offense by joking about it. "I tell them, 'This is your wicked stepmother,' " said a stepmother of three boys. "Clean your rooms and I'll turn into a fairy godmother who will take you to the movies." Others advise talking freely about the myth so you defuse its power to hurt.

▪ THIS TIME IT'S FOREVER ▪

While it seems that love is better the second time around, the hard truth is that according to researchers, sixty percent of second marriages fail. What's more, the number one reason for the failure of a second marriage to work out is claimed to be "the kids."

> A divorcee with no children married a man with two young teenage sons. "I was delighted to have kids at last," she said. "I was determined that we'd make it as a family. I tried. I really did. But his kids felt his father had brought in a live-in maid, not a wife. They lived like pigs and expected me to clean up after them. When I complained to my husband, he just laughed and said, "Boys will be boys." He said I was too compulsive when I asked if they'd at least put the dirty dishes in the kitchen so I could put them in the dishwasher. I finally decided it really wasn't worth it anymore. I had given the marriage three years and nothing had changed. I got out. So much for stepmotherhood."

Know what you're getting into before you say, "I do." Don't be discouraged by the statistics. Even though sixty percent of re-marriages end in divorce, that means forty percent work out. Mine did. My second husband and I have been married 37 years. So it does happen. Think positively. Be one of the forty percent. Maybe even those odds will improve as we move into the twenty-first century.

▪ MYTH: STEPFAMILIES ARE NO DIFFERENT ▪ FROM BIOLOGICAL FAMILIES

If that were true, you wouldn't be reading this book. Stepfamilies *are* different; not bad or abnormal, just different. Stepfamilies are created through pain and out of a loss, either by a divorce or by death. A blended family's foundation is built over the ashes of memories—some good, some bad—of another marriage. If that marriage ended in divorce, there is sadness and regret for the dream of the perfect family that failed to materialize. If the former marriage was ended by a partner's death, there are bound to be echoes of a past remembered, especially at "marker" times such as holidays, birthdays, births, and other life-cycle events.

In addition to the emotional baggage of past recollections on the part of the biological parent and children, a stepparent enters into a family scene that is already formed. Although the entire orig-inal team is no longer present, the remaining members have been playing the game for awhile and know each other's moves, moods, and memories. The stepparent starts out cold, without knowledge of the family history, inside jokes, references about deceased pets or previous vacations, let alone food and movie preferences. Even the family's unique idioms are unfamiliar. The game's lopsided from the get-go. Bring to this unlevel playing field a few stepsi-blings who also don't know the score or even what game is being played, and you'll quickly understand why stepfamilies are differ-ent.

This doesn't mean to say that all is hopeless. On the contrary, integration can and usually does occur and a team spirit prevails. But this blending of families doesn't happen without awareness of the pitfalls, without patience, without strong communication skills, and without a strong sense of humor to pad the falls.

▪ MYTH: A STEPPARENT IS A "STAND-IN" PARENT ▪

A stepparent is not like a module that can be snapped into place when an old part dies, malfunctions, or needs updating. A stepparent is his or her own unique entity, not a different model of or a newer product of the same thing.

Wise stepparents don't try to define what they are, other than to say, "I'm your mom's husband," or "I'm your dad's wife." Instead they say what they are not: "I'm not a replacement for your own mother/father. I'm not trying to take his/her place in your life."

▪ MYTH: BECAUSE YOU LOVE YOUR SPOUSE, ▪ YOU'LL IMMEDIATELY LOVE YOUR STEPCHILDREN

Nope. It doesn't happen, at least it didn't to even one of the more than one hundred interviews I conducted for this book. Love, like flowers, grows with the passage of time, with an abundance of tenderness, care, and the wisdom to know when to stand back and let nature take its course. You can't rush love, especially with kids who have been hurt by their parent's divorce or by the death of a parent.

They really don't trust a newcomer right away. Are you trying to fill their mother or father's shoes? How will you change their lives? Will their parent love you more than them? If they let down their guard and do begin to form a relationship, will you leave too?

You too may have doubts and fears. The toddlers may be cute and cuddly, but when they don't feel well, they cry out for their "real" mommy or daddy. The adolescents may be nice, but often sassy. If you've never had kids, you really aren't sure if it's just a developmental stage or if they really dislike you, so it's hard not to take their moods personally.

How can love develop? By going slowly, just as you would when you meet a new person or even a strange dog. Let the kids get a sense of you. Be yourself, not some image of what you think they want you to be. Be there for them without trying to overwhelm or take charge. Ask for their input, but don't take it personally if they shrug and walk away. Listen more than you talk. It all doesn't have to happen the first day, first month, or even first year.

■ **MYTH: EVERYONE IN A STEPFAMILY GETS ALONG** ■
WITH EACH OTHER FROM DAY ONE

This is the flip side of the wicked stepparent myth. This fantasy is created by the movies, stage shows, and television sitcoms such as *The Brady Bunch*, *The Sound of Music*, and *Yours, Mine, and Ours*, and others where the stepparent and stepsiblings are welcomed with open arms, where there is no jealousy, no fighting, and no hurt feelings. There also is no truth in this picture for stepfamilies or biological families either, for that matter.

Everyone must be patient. It takes time for blended families to work out all of the lumps. New experiences are difficult for some people, especially children who have been hurt by their parent's divorce or by having one of their parents die. Just when you take a sigh of relief and think things are going beautifully, a crisis may develop. Take solace in knowing that this is standard operating procedure for biological families, too. No one ever said raising kids—yours, his/hers, or both of yours—was easy. It's somewhat akin to taking a car trip with your loved one on a rugged road. Sometimes the scenery is so breathtaking and the conversation so stimulating that you forget to notice the bumps; other times, you shake a lot.

▪ MYTH: THE KIDS ARE BETTER OFF WITH YOUR ▪ EX-SPOUSE TOTALLY OUT OF THE PICTURE

Most experts agree that except for rare situations where contact with your ES puts the children in harm's way, your kids are better off seeing their other biological parent. If he or she really is a bum, you're better off letting the youngster gradually form his or her own opinion rather than forbidding a relationship. The same advice goes for dealing with any extended family members that were close to the children before the end of your former marriage. Chapters Two and Four both deal with how to handle relationships (and relations) from a former marriage.

Why shouldn't you protect your children from your former spouse, especially after the way he or she treated you and the kids? Because if either the stepparent or biological parent refuses or makes it difficult for children to see their biological parent, chances are the kids will rebel. You'll end up being the bad guy. (Obviously, if there were any type of abuse—physical, sexual, or verbal—involved, you should discuss this situation with a qualified counselor, before permitting the children to make contact.)

▪ MYTH: IF THE KIDS HAVE PROBLEMS, ▪ IT'S BECAUSE YOU'RE A BLENDED FAMILY

Many people would like to use this as an excuse, but it isn't true. Kids with both biological parents living in the same home in a seemingly happy marriage also have problems. It's being human, being a youngster, and learning how to grow up. Stop feeling guilty and begin to work with your child, letting him or her know that the important word in the phrase, "blended family" is "family." As a family, you will work things out. This fall-back security is what's important, even if the youngster can't put it into words as you would like.

▪ MYTH: TIME ALONE WILL WORK THINGS OUT ▪

Although time does cure many things, time alone often cannot alleviate some of the problems that arise in a blended family. Don't try to go it alone. You'll not only dig yourselves a deeper hole, but you'll be creating such resentment and frustrations that it will take longer to finally reach any sort of comfort level.

There are many warm and caring therapists and counselors who are experienced in helping blended families work out difficulties. Begin by contacting your rabbi, minister, or priest. If your clergy person is not specially trained to help, he or she can give you names of a psychologist, psychiatrist, social worker, or guidance counselor who is qualified. If the therapy is not covered by your insurance, call the Jewish Family Services, Catholic Family Services, or the social service organization for your particular religious organization. These groups usually offer their therapy services with payment on a sliding scale.

> "I never went to a stepparenting group," said a mother with one stepson, a son by a former marriage, and a child from her present marriage. "We did, however, seek the help of two family counselors while putting our family together. I feel that was a MUST. I don't know if we'd be together had we not . . . We had the kids talk privately to the counselors to make sure they were doing okay. We were guided to move slowly and carefully into structuring our new family, with the kids as active participants and their voices and hearts heard. We did the best we could and I think it was of great benefit to all. We still periodically see the last psychologist to make sure the kids continue to do well, that we don't miss something we'll regret later. My son also has asked to see the "talking doctor" sometimes when things are rough with his dad."

Continue to see the therapist, even though immediate problems may have been solved. Urge your children to let you know when they feel the need to talk to an objective outsider. This is a situation when an ounce of prevention is truly worth a pound of cure.

• MYTH: WE DON'T NEED ANY OUTSIDE HELP •

This is not the time to circle the wagons. You *do* need to let outsiders inside your magic circle. However, professional counselors are not the only source of help for blended families. Many stepfamilies have turned to support groups, both on-line and those offered by their church or synagogue. Support groups reassure you that "nothing's new under the sun." The problems or difficulties you and your blended family may be facing are probably very similar to those experienced by other families. These "experts" can share positive ways in which they solved or circumvented these issues. One caveat, however: If you find yourselves in a group that seems more interested in griping and complaining than problem solving, look for another that is more constructive.

Peer support groups can also offer a great deal of comfort to adolescents, who quickly learn that their blended family is not so unusual after all. That alone can be quite a relief at an age where "being different" is tantamount to total extinction. Pre-teens and teens will usually listen to peers, even when they seem to rebel against talking to adults. At peer support meetings adolescents may discover tips for adjusting to stepsiblings, sharing a room while still maintaining a modicum of privacy, getting used to a stepparent, and learning how to live in two households while always knowing where you are.

Outside help in the form of child care assistance is also vital to the well-being of a blended family. Both stepparent and spouse need to arrange for time together to nurture their marriage, strong insurance for creating a happy blended family. More on this subject is found in Chapter Twelve.

• MYTH: IF YOU FOLLOW CERTAIN SET RULES, • YOUR BLENDED FAMILY WILL HAVE NO DIFFICULTIES

Regretfully, there isn't a set of "Ten Commandments" for settling in as a stepfamily. Each unit is as unique as its members. What might work perfectly for you could create a disaster for someone else. While that means you can't get a map with specific directions to keep you out of the woods, you can follow certain tracks to keep you out of any quicksand.

Check your favorite bookstore or library for the names of books (such as this one) and locate stepfamily support groups with special sessions for youngsters of all ages, including adult children who suddenly find themselves in a stepfamily. These peer groups help in that you find others with similar problems and can learn what worked (or didn't work). It also sometimes helps just to know that others have walked in your shoes, even if your terrain may differ slightly.

Many stepfamilies admitted that their greatest help was from therapy sessions (both individual and as a family) with a qualified therapist who was experienced in dealing with blended family issues. This person could be a psychologist, psychiatrist, social worker, or a member of the clergy.

■   MYTH: THE WORST IS BEHIND US NOW;   ■
     OUR BLENDED FAMILY IS RUNNING SMOOTHLY

No relationship is ever lump-free. Relationships are ever-changing and those that include children are even more so. Every developmental stage brings with it new problems. That's not to say that these problems are insurmountable. Difficulties certainly can be smoothed out, but the couple who sit back, smiling benignly, thinking that they can coast on their marriage or family relationships are due for some nasty surprises.

You need to keep working on those skills that have made your marriage successful, as well as those that have blended your two families into one that is functioning well. Good communication is always at the forefront of these skills. Don't wait for problems to arise before dusting off your communication skills. Keep them fresh and alive by using them on a daily basis. Listen to your children as they grow and develop, moving gradually from one stage to another, shedding dependence for independence and struggling to maintain confidence and a sense of self-esteem as they waver from the beginnings of maturity to wanting (now and then) to reach back to the safety of home, the very one you and your spouse have created with your blended family.

CHAPTER TWELVE

Adults Only

"A successful marriage is an edifice that must be rebuilt every day."

—ANDRE MAUROIS
(pseudonym of Emile Salomon Wilheim Herzog)
French author

*I*t's easy for stepparents to remain so focused on the kids they both may have brought into their blended family that they overlook the real reason why they got together in the first place: They love each other. The old saying, "The best gift a man can give his children is to love their mother," holds true in stepfamilies as well. But a love that is grounded in friendship, mutual respect, confidence in one another, fidelity, honesty, and caring doesn't just happen. It takes energy and effort to develop, time and patience to grow.

Unfortunately, energy, effort, time, and patience are in short demand when a couple is dealing with his, her, and our kids and their respective comings and goings; work schedules; running a household; caring for elderly parents; volunteer work, and all the other pressures and responsibilities inherent in today's lifestyle.

Often, however, one of the major triggers of stress is the kids. This isn't just true in stepfamilies. It happens in biological families, too. The only arguments my husband and I have ever had in over thirty-seven years of marriage centered on some aspect of dealing with our five kids.

But in stepfamilies, tensions are stretched even tighter as spouses try to get stepsiblings to adjust to the new living environment, learn to deal with the kids' other parent, and get acclimated to living with someone else's kids. It's not easy. Unfortunately, difficulty with kids is a major reason the majority of parents in blended families give for breaking up.

"I didn't have any kids of my own," a newspaperwoman in Mississippi said. "So I was looking forward to having some, even if they were stepchildren. I tried to make it work for two years, but his teenage daughters would have no part of it. They were rude to me, made fun of my attempts to cook, and refused to help clean the house or share any other responsibilities. I felt like their maid, not a stepmother. I grew to hate them and, after awhile, I hated him, too, for not supporting me emotionally against their abuse. I'm getting a divorce, my second. It isn't the way I would have liked this marriage to have worked out, but I know it's for the best."

In some cases, you have to do the best you can. No one can be expected to do more than that. Remember that you married your spouse because you loved him or her. The kids offer an extra dimension that may or may not become an asset. As one stepmother sadly advised, "Sometimes you have to do your best and just accept the fact that maybe some of your stepkids won't ever really like you. It's too bad, but it's reality."

▪ BOND WITH YOUR SPOUSE ▪

The reason you remarried probably was primarily because you loved your spouse. Only secondary, if at all, was your wanting to have a partner to help you raise your kids or agreeing to raise his or hers. Remember why you married. That motive tends to fall in back of the dresser when you aren't careful, collecting dust until it's time to move on. And then it's too late. Adopt my philosophy of marriage, which is really very simple: Your spouse comes first. One day (God willing), the kids will grow up and leave you. If, by that time, the two of you haven't made the effort to develop a strong relationship and closeness, the kids' departure will leave two strangers alone in the house.

Too often in blended families the husband/wife relationship takes a backseat in the couple's well-meaning attempt to make things as normal as possible for the children and stepchildren.

Fueled by guilt, the adults become so busy trying to make their
kids feel secure that they neglect each other and grow apart. Their
action—or rather, inaction—nullifies what they were trying to ac-
complish in the first place: offering their kids a secure family life.
The stronger your marriage bonds are forged, the more agile you
and your spouse will become in pulling together to solve problems
with your kids, as well as with what life tosses your way. Never
underestimate the strength you both possess when you're united
in a binding love.

STRENGTHEN COMMUNICATION SKILLS

Chapter Three deals with the ways in which you can strengthen
communication skills as a family. But communication also must
flow easily between a couple because you both have many issues
to work out behind the scenes in order to present a united front
to the kids. The more comfortable you both become in communicating openly and honestly, the easier it becomes to show your
kids by example the importance you place on communication.

Never stop reaching out to your spouse to develop and nourish
your communication skills because this is one of the most important gifts you can give to one another to keep your marriage
healthy and growing. Even after thirty-seven years of marriage, my
husband and I never seem to be at a loss for things to talk about.
It may be as mundane as rehashing a football game or discussing
a movie we both enjoyed—or that one liked and the other didn't.
We bring to each other's attention a beautiful sunset or the sight
of a white seagull sitting on the lawn in Maine, waiting for his daily
bribe of bread crumbs. We share the silent language of the soul as
well, that wonderful transmission of thoughts that communicates
completely when two marital partners have joined minds as well
as bodies.

MAKE TIME TO COMMUNICATE WITH ONE ANOTHER

Most couples talk to each other, but if you recorded their conversation, you'd find that it was mostly "grasshopper talk," jump-

ing from one topic to another without focus. It's hopping from who's taking the car pool to what dry cleaners is least likely to melt the shirt buttons to what should be done about the faucet that's still leaking. This is necessary talk, but it does nothing to further the goals of the marriage, to advance or improve your relationship, or to share real feelings with the person you love. You need to make time for that.

But time alone for true communication doesn't take place by accident. You both must agree on its importance and be willing to make the time to talk without interruptions from the kids, the telephone, drop-in guests, or television. This special time together must be taken seriously and treated with respect. It must take place on a regular basis, not just when you think about it. Get up half an hour earlier and talk over coffee before the kids get up. Retire the automatic dishwasher and talk as you wash and dry the dishes. Go out on the porch and talk before or after dinner. Or take a bath together before going to bed and use that as your time for talking. As a friend observed, "more couples take time to floss each day than to talk to each other. They'll have great teeth, but who will notice?"

SET A REGULAR "DATE NIGHT"

One way to make time to really communicate with one another is to schedule a regular "date night." Even if one or both of you spend one night a week out with the guys or gals, you need to allot an additional night a week to go out together as a couple. It may be the only time you have all week to enjoy each other's company as man and wife, rather than parent and stepparent. You probably did it *before* you two got married. Why end it after saying, "I do?"

When our five children were small, my husband and I had a standing Wednesday night date, with each other. We had a permanent baby-sitter lined up for that evening so we *had* to go somewhere. Often we planned nothing more than a quiet dinner at a nice restaurant with no one spilling milk or needing his or her meat cut up. Our only rule—which we frequently broke—was "no talking about the kids."

Where we went on our "date" was really not as important as the fact that we recognized that our relationship as man and wife had a top priority. Marriage is a lot like sterling silver; if you don't keep polishing it, it tarnishes a little. We determined right from the beginning that our marriage would continue to shine, even after the original glow was well worn by years of loving caresses, as well as numerous unanticipated dents and dings.

For many blended families who don't have "our" children, the "date night" is taken care of by joint custody. In those cases, the biological parent may only have his or her child every other week or only during specific days of each week. Use that time of the "off week" to rejuvenate your marriage bond. Have a romantic dinner out, cuddle up with a pizza and each other and watch old movies on television, or go sailing, hiking, biking, fishing, or sit and watch the sunset together. There's something special about enjoying nature together with someone you love.

> A newly married stepfather, whose wife had her child with her every other week, remarked honestly, "It helps to have some time alone with my bride without her child always being around. It gives us time to bond as a couple on those days so we have a stronger partnership on the days we're parenting."

Other stepparents who had no children of their own but had married someone with kids echoed this thought. For those couples who also had children together, the joint custody arrangement offered them some special time to spend just with their "our" children.

DO YOUR ARGUING BACKSTAGE

There may be times when the two of you don't agree on specific matters. Actually, it's quite unlikely that you'll agree with your spouse on every issue, especially when it involves the kids, regardless if they're yours, his, or both of yours. But do your fighting offstage, so your audiences (the kids or the grandparents) aren't witnesses. You'll frighten the kids who may think another divorce is in the works, and make the grandparents both uncomfortable and ready to take sides.

It isn't that you want your kids to think couples never argue. On the contrary, children who never see their parent and stepparent disagree have unrealistic ideas about the give and take required in marriages. But you need to present a united front on major issues, so do your battling backstage. Set up fair fighting rules in advance, so you can work these issues out amicably.

Stipulate that you'll agree on a proper time and place to talk even if that means postponing the discussion until later. Standing in the kitchen following your father's birthday dinner with the company still there is neither the right time nor place. Don't try to settle disagreements during television commercials or at bedtime either. Your bed should be for sleeping and making love, not arguing. And, of course, never go to bed angry.

Instead, when you think an issue is going to be controversial or may have more than one way it can be settled, find a neutral spot to talk. Go for a walk in the park, do "a Seinfeld" and meet at the local coffee shop, or go into the living room or another room where you can shut the door and not be overheard by the kids. If you go walking in the park, you'll use up physical energy and should burn off some of your emotion so you can disagree without getting angry. Having coffee in a public place also reminds you to discuss your disagreements civilly.

If your battle zone is going to be at home, free yourself of distractions. Let the telephone machine answer your calls. Use the kitchen timer to set a time limit so you both know you have a closing limit. Otherwise, you can waste an entire evening wandering off the point or repeating yourselves. If, however, at the end of the time limit one or both of you feel you have more information to share before making a decision, agree to extend the time limit.

If either of you feel you don't have time to discuss the issues because you have a case to prepare for the next day or you promised the kids you'd help with homework, set up a specific time when you will be available and stick to that appointment.

Once you do get together, remember to focus on the issue at hand. Agree in the beginning what you'll be discussing, even if you have to write down an agenda. Both of you should have input into what goes on the list.

Don't bring in outside concerns or yesterday's frustrations. It's easy to pad your points when you're still frustrated that your spouse's ex was late returning his or her kid, which made you late for your night class or that you had to handle the last two house repairs and that wasn't supposed to be your job. Unless those are the issues you've agreed to discuss, stifle the urge to sneak those complaints in.

If you're like me, you forget what you wanted to say when you get emotional. It's hard to defend your point of view when you can't recall any of the particulars. Go ahead and make a cheat sheet if you need to.

Remember that the object of arguing with your spouse is to reach agreement or compromise on an issue. It is not supposed to be a fight to the death. Couples who forget their fair fighting rules often end up with the death of the marriage, or at least one that is bloody and bent. If that isn't want you want, use these fair fighting tips to make your arguments more persuasive:

1. Give "I" messages.

Tell your spouse how you feel by saying, "I feel ganged up on when you don't support what I've said in front of the kids," or "I feel angry and frustrated when no one helps me clean up after dinner."

2. Avoid saying, "You always . . ." or "You never . . ."

But do say what action you *would* like, such as, "I'd like you to support me in front of the kids," or "I'd like you or the kids to help me clean up after dinner." Your spouse probably doesn't read minds.

3. Attack the issue, not the person.

Attack the issue that upsets you by saying, "I'm tired of picking up your dirty clothes up off the floor," not "You're an inconsiderate slob."

4. Make your request known in an unemotional manner.

Express it by saying, "I'd like you to make an effort to be home in time for dinner," not "If you loved me, you'd be home in time for dinner."

DEMAND PRIVACY IN YOUR BEDROOM

Virginia Woolf said that every woman needed "a room of her own." I believe every married couple also needs a room of their own, a haven from the kids, a place conducive to conversation as well as intimacy, a retreat with a lock. For most of us, that room is called the bedroom.

While there's nothing wrong with having the kids coming in and piling on the bed on Sunday morning to read the comics with the adults, the bedroom should be known as the parent's refuge, with guests entering only by knocking or being invited in.

This courtesy not only teaches the children to accept and respect their parent and stepparent as a couple, but it also reinforces the need for everyone to respect one another's privacy. (By the same token, parents need to knock at their children's door and wait for admittance.)

As a single parent, you or your spouse may have permitted the kids to come in during the night and crawl into bed. Now, in the early months of a remarriage, you may find your kids or your spouse's kids resenting the new "our bedroom" rules. If you hear the patter of little feet at night, you or your spouse (depending on whose kids they are) need to get up and give the youngster a reassuring hug, remind the child of the new rules now that Mommy or Daddy is married, and firmly take the son or daughter back to bed. Expect this to be an issue for awhile. But if you aren't consistent, it can grow into a major problem.

ESTABLISH A SENSE OF TRUST

If one or both of you have been married before, you may still
be nursing bruises from the former marriage, especially when it
comes to the issue of trust. Discuss this between yourselves and
talk about the areas where you still feel vulnerable. Tell your
spouse, "If you're late coming home and don't call, I start thinking,
'Oh, no, is it happening to me again?' " or "I appreciate your telling me when you're going out to lunch with your co-worker (of
the opposite sex), but I guess it makes me feel a little jealous and
somewhat scared. Let's talk about what would make me feel less
anxious."

By revealing to your spouse what fears still linger from "before," you have shown your trust and opened the way to real communication. Never expect your new marital partner to be a mind
reader. He or she may truly be a marvel, but mind reading probably isn't one of the virtues.

There are risks in loving again and risks in sharing our secrets,
but those who never risk anything never achieve anything either.
When you open yourself to trust another person and that person
does the same to you, the rewards are wonderful and well worth
the risk.

• BE WILLING TO COMPROMISE WITHOUT •
FEELING YOU'VE LOST

When you have reached out to one another and achieved a
sense of trust and strengthened communication skills, you begin
to feel that as a team you can conquer all—the ES, in-laws, your
boss, and even the paper delivery person who insists on throwing
your paper into the bushes.

One important part of achieving that touching of souls is to be
able to make compromises without feeling that you have "lost."
In a strong marriage, there is no win/lose scoreboard, but rather a
compromise quotient that says the marriage is the real winner.
When that occurs, the rippling effect also touches your kids and
everyone whose life impacts yours. Yes, even your spouse's ex.

Ask yourself if a particular issue is really that important to you. If it is, try to analyze why it is. In some situations, you may have a particularly strong view, such as expecting your stepchildren to show you respect even if they disagree with you. Hopefully, chances are your spouse would agree with you as well.

If, however, your spouse has a vacation coming up and he or she wants to spend it with the kids while you want a romantic getaway, each of you may have to present your views and then arrive at a satisfying compromise. One such solution could be sharing a few days with the kids and then spending the rest of the week together as a couple.

Discipline is another area where compromise is a necessity in blended families. One of you may be more laid-back while the other is a stickler for rules. But the kids are used to their former house rules. Add onto that the rules that you want established in your stepfamily, which may or may not be enforced in the kids' other parents' homes. While it's fine to let kids know that there are different rules in different houses, make sure to present a united front in the one house you really care about: your home. You and your spouse need to discuss your rules for discipline and agree on whatever compromises as may be necessary. Then stick to them. Consistency is important.

You may find that once you develop your compromise abilities with your spouse, you can negotiate more comfortably with an ES as well. Once you understand that there doesn't need to be a winner and a loser, but rather two adults working out a problem to a mutually satisfying solution, you'll become more objective and have less emotional baggage to sort through. Perhaps you'll even show your ES how easy it is to reach a common ground for the good of the kids.

The most gratifying aspect of learning to compromise is that your kids will see you in action and observe that when two people each give a little, a bond gets stronger, not weaker. That's an important lesson to learn at any age, but certainly one that can help your kids get through their difficult adolescent and teen years more comfortably. There's no doubt that the "promise" in compromise offers you and your spouse more potential happiness in your future together.

▪ BRING LAUGHTER INTO YOUR MARRIAGE ▪

You've probably already discovered that in blended families you have to "hit the ground running." There's no time to sleep in on weekends and reflect on the romance of the wedding because you already have the kids around. Many couples forgo the honeymoon altogether, or if they do go away, they take their kids with them.

There are many stresses when you're trying to blend two families and minimize the lumps. But by using one of the most important of our senses, the sense of humor, you and your spouse can ease many of the problems in your blended family. Laughter lightens a mood, making discussion flow more comfortably. As you'll learn in Chapter Thirteen, laughter can help to reduce stress as well. It brightens our outlook when things seem dark and builds a sense of trust. Use laughter to deepen your relationship with your spouse. Find fun in your lives together, in the absurdities and the sad things too. Once again, your kids will pick up on what they see. Laughter makes us all feel better. As pianist/entertainer Victor Borge is credited with saying, "Laughter is the shortest distance between two people."

▪ LET YOUR KIDS SEE YOU SHOW ▪ SIGNS OF LOVE AND RESPECT

While it's important to let the kids see you both showing signs of love and respect to one another, be discreet in showing physical affection in public. Kids will usually let you know when you've crossed over their comfort zone. If you hear them complaining, "Mom and Joe are always hugging and kissing. It's disgusting," or "Can't you and Dad ever stop acting like teenagers?" chances are you've embarrassed them or made them feel disloyal to their other parent.

Adolescents, teenagers, and even adult children often feel uncomfortable when faced with their parents' sexuality. It makes no difference whether their parents are divorced or if the other parent has died. A twenty-five year-old man, whose father had been dead for eight years, told me, "I'm glad Mom's dating now. I don't want her to be lonesome. But then, I don't want to hear about her dates either."

Use your common sense and remember that you are constantly demonstrating by example how you and your spouse respect and care for one another. Don't joke at the other's expense or make demeaning or sarcastic remarks. Don't use sexual innuendos in front of the kids either. Illustrate to your children how two responsible adults interact with one another. Our kids are probably the best mimes in the world. Let them mimic our love for one another. What we do speaks so loudly they can't hear what we say.

CHAPTER THIRTEEN

Reducing Stress

"Complete freedom from stress is death."

—HANS SELYE
endocrinologist

▪ DEFINITION OF STRESS ▪

Stress is best defined as "a state of bodily or mental tension resulting from factors that tend to alter an existent equilibrium."[1]

There are many "factors that tend to alter an existent equilibrium" in blended families. It begins with the marriage of two adults, with one or both bringing children, to whom change in itself can be stressful, to the newly created family. In addition, the new blended family home may be physically too small for all those bodies to find any privacy and emotionally too filled with memories of a former marriage. A different cooking style or eating habits may alienate whichever part of the family that isn't used to them. Differing personalities and individuals with different histories need time to connect, while money issues and discipline techniques must be worked out. No wonder one's "existent equilibrium" is altered when a blended family is created.

But all stress isn't necessarily of a negative nature. Many stressful situations can actually give us great happiness and satisfaction, such as getting married, moving into a larger and more comfortable house, seeing your stepchildren perform on stage or on the athletic field, or taking a family vacation. Stress also can be triggered by imagined events that never come to pass. About fifteen percent of the population are chronic worriers, wasting what could be productive time and energy by worrying, an activity that actually

---

[1]*Webster's Ninth New Collegiate Dictionary*, (Springfield, MA, 1986), Merriam-Webster, Inc. Publishers.

interferes with thought processes and creates additional stress. While stress can be triggered by happy, troublesome, and even imagined events, too much uncontrolled stress can have harmful effects, both physically and mentally, on an individual as well as an entire family. What's important, according to the late Dr. Hans Selye, a world-famous pioneer in the study of the effects of stress, is that "Stress depends not upon what happens to an individual but upon the way he reacts."

In their often quoted 1967 study, The Holmes–Rahe Social Readjustment Scale, psychiatrists Thomas H. Holmes and Richard H. Rahe, of the University of Washington Medical School devised a ranking of more than forty stressful events, assigning points to each of them. Some of the events were positive ones, such as getting married or enjoying great personal achievement. Others were more negative, such as being fired, getting divorced, or the death of a spouse. Some could be considered neutral, their interpretation dependent on each person's unique situation, such as pregnancy, gaining a new family member, or holidays such as Christmas. Drs. Holmes and Rahe's findings indicated that a person's vulnerability to illness could be predicted fairly accurately according to how they scored.

But you shouldn't "sweat the little things" either. In 1981, researcher Richard Lazarus, Ph.D., professor of psychiatry at the University of California at Berkeley and his colleagues concluded a study that weighed the effects of what they called "hassles," the everyday "minor" irritations of life. Their conclusion: "continual daily events such as those caused by too much responsibility and constant interruptions can adversely affect an individual, eventually creating even more stress than a single traumatic life event."

These two studies demonstrate that the mental and physical health of all those involved in blended families is vulnerable to the effects of stress. You must acknowledge whatever causes stress within your own home (as well as in your work), and begin to identify how you respond to those stressors. Then you must initiate steps described in this chapter to negate the power stress holds over you and your family.

THE PERCEPTION OF STRESS AFFECTS YOUR REALITY

Each of us has a different threshold for stress, and this level can vary, depending on how we are feeling at the time. If you haven't slept well the night before or are fighting a cold or the flu, you may find the kids' fighting highly stressful, whereas your usual reaction is to tell them to take it outside. When you're feeling stressed and the stepchildren complain about your cooking, saying it isn't as good as their "real" mother's (or father's), you may burst into tears or throw the casserole on the floor, rather than making a joke or telling them that they can cook tomorrow.

A youngster may become anxious the night before going to the other parent's house because the stepsibs there are rough and boisterous or because he or she doesn't like the stepparent there.

Because we're all different and our reactions to stress also vary, you might find your kids' and stepkids' clutter very stressful, while your spouse, their laid-back stepfather/stepmother may think you're being obsessive about neatness. The noise level of your blended household may create additional stress for one or both of you. Stepparents who had no children of their own and were used to quiet or at most, the stereo on in the background especially mentioned noise as being very stressful. I am compulsive about promptness and find it very stressful to have to wait for people. I try to reduce my self-induced stress by bringing a book or postcards with me so I can be "busy" rather than just fuming.

THE DANGERS OF UNCONTROLLED STRESS

If you don't learn to control the negative stress in your life, both at home in your blended family as well as in your work and even volunteer activities, you will pay a high price since stress wears down the immune system. Many physical ailments such as hypertension, heart attacks, strokes, sexual dysfunction, migraines, cardiovascular disease, stiff neck, backaches, arthritis, asthma, accidents, diarrhea, depression, the common cold, irritable bowel syndrome, and even cancer may be traced to the relentless corrosive nature of stress. Although each person's "breaking point" differs and some people even insist they are "addicted to adrenaline," stress, even the "good" kind, can eventually wear us down. Stress is a lot like rainfall. A little isn't harmful and often is good, but too many drops eventually erode even the hardest granite.

I know firsthand that negative stress, what Dr. Hans Selye called "dis-stress," can take its toll and that often it is the cause of accidents. I was extremely close to my younger brother. When he was in the hospital with terminal colon cancer, I was devastated. One day after visiting him, I came home and decided to clean out one of my sons' closets. (I deal with stress by becoming overly busy.) Noticing a can of white spray paint sitting on a shelf, I reached for the can and began to spray the closet shelves, thinking I'd "freshen them up a bit." It was a big mistake. In such close quarters, the paint spray flew back in my eyes. Along with everything else I was dealing with, I had to be treated for chemical conjunctivitis. The moral: Do less when you're under stress because you can be accident-prone.

▪ BE AWARE OF "AWFULIZING" ▪

This wonderful term "awfulizing" comes from psychologist and author Albert Ellis. Most of us do it from time to time. It means creating a scenario of awful things that could happen and piling them one on top of the other until we feel totally overwhelmed and stressed out.

Many parents do that before they have even a minor confrontation with their ES. It goes something like this. "My ex left a message for me to call her. It probably means she wants more money. Or maybe she's going to say that I can't take the kids to the beach next weekend because she has plans. She's going to get my kids upset because they've been looking forward to the beach and that means they'll be impossible to handle . . ." Well, you get the idea. Nothing's even happened yet, and the awfulizer is already angry and traumatized by the possibilities.

It would be vastly more helpful if this father, rather than awfulizing, would visualize a pleasant conversation with his ex-wife so that when he returned the call, he wasn't tense or hostile. Often, by imagining the worst, we create far more problems in reality due to our behavior. Think about it next time you start piling "awfuls" on top of one another. Some experts even suggest setting aside a short period every day to worry and then forbidding yourself to worry any more that day. I prefer to go the positive route by visualizing things working out just the way I want them to and often they do. Power of positive thinking.

▪ CHILDREN/STEPCHILDREN USE PARENTS/STEPPARENTS ▪ AS ROLE MODELS IN DEALING WITH STREES

Kids are born mimics. We know they ape our bad points when we hear them repeating things we wish we hadn't said or demonstrating inappropriate behaviors we know they've learned from us. But they can learn to copy our good points, too, which is why it is so important to learn to cope with stress so you can teach them by example. There is an old saying: "Children may close their ears to advice, but open their eyes to example."

TALK TO THE KIDS ABOUT WAYS TO HANDLE STRESS

You need to keep talking about the various ways to handle stress, especially at family meetings or when you're one-on-one with your child and you know he or she is feeling the pressures of stress. Be an understanding listener, too. Your youngster may give you clues as to what is so stressful. You may even find that you share some of the same stressors, such as too much noise, lack of privacy, or too many activities for too little time. It can draw a stepparent and stepchild closer together as they work out a joint solution. While the best way to demonstrate the myriad techniques for coping with stress is by actions, not words, freely share with your kids the techniques you've used for reducing the stress in your life and invite them to join you. You'll help your stepkids feel more in control of their lives by helping them learn to cope with their stress.

Teenagers often cope with stress by listening to music, talking to friends, running, and getting away from their parents. Let them know that you understand that their coping techniques may be different from yours, but encourage them to try some of the stress reduction techniques listed in this chapter.

RECOGNIZE THE SIGNS OF STRESS

What we now call "stress" is the same automatic biological response that kept our cave-dwelling ancestors alive. When closing in for the kill, escaping from hostile neighboring clans or wild animals, or fighting nature, their nervous systems shut down their digestive systems and increased their oxygen consumption, heart rate, and blood pressure. This hormonal reaction, what physiologist Walter B. Cannon called the "fight or flight" response, had a definite purpose for primitive man and still does for military personnel engaged in battle, athletes, and others needing to fight or escape. Most of us, however, trigger the same hormonal reaction over lesser demands and have no release for this response. Stress builds up and eventually affects us adversely physically or emotionally.

It's not too hard to tell when people are feeling too much stress, even if they don't want to talk about it. Their behavior may change. A typically even-tempered youngster suddenly storms out of the room, slamming the door. A usually healthy spouse does a morning "body count," complaining of vague symptoms of not feeling well, such as a tension headache, intestinal upset, or tight shoulders the day of a meeting with the ex-mate is scheduled. Uptight teens tap their fingers, jingle the coins in their pockets, or sigh. Others may appear restless, grind or clench their teeth, binge or refuse to eat, have sweaty palms, become angry at the slightest provocation, or complain of rapidheart beat or light-headedness.

TEACH KIDS THAT STRESS IS PART OF LIFE

While it's tempting to think you can help your children and stepchildren avoid stress altogether, you not only can't, you shouldn't even try. Stress is a part of life. When you overprotect children, they not only fail to recognize the signs of stress, but they also never learn the techniques that will help them deal with stress.

There's no doubt that today's youngsters face many stresses in their lives. Our media is filled with images of pencil-thin bodies for women and muscular ones for men. Youthful actors or models seem never to suffer from acne, awkwardness, or any of the other problems your own kids may face. They may worry about their own body image, fearing that they don't "measure up" to whatever seems to be the norm. Studies show that girls are more likely than boys to suffer from lowered self-esteem as they enter puberty. This may be one reason that more girls than boys suffer from eating disorders or why there is a growing number of girls as young as eight who think of themselves as "fat" and are on some type of self-imposed diet.

Many youngsters are under stress to maintain a specific low weight, such as ballet dancers, wrestlers, gymnasts, and models. Adolescent boys on football or hockey teams, are often told by coaches that they must "bulk up."

Boys who are not athletic also suffer from self-imposed stress, feeling that they are not macho enough to get girls to like them, while those who are athletic worry just as much about their competitiveness, how they stack up to the other players. A poor showing can frustrate a youngster trying to make the team and who fears he may be cut. Stress lowers self-esteem just at a time a young person needs to have a strong sense of confidence.

Then, too, it takes some children longer than others to adjust to change, and certainly changes abound for a child who has suddenly acquired a stepparent, stepsiblings, and may be in a new home and/or school. A new baby in the family also can create stress in youngsters, especially the youngest who may be losing the valued position as "baby of the family." Be watchful during these changes in the kids' lives and encourage them to talk about their feelings regarding them.

Many children suffer from silent fears—that there'll be another divorce bringing with it more changes, that the biological parent may die, that they may not be liked or accepted by the stepparent, or that the biological parent will love a baby born to the "new family" more than them.

▪ CHECKING YOUR STRESS LEVEL ▪

BODY CHECK

Some people live under a perpetual umbrella of stress and don't even recognize the signs in themselves. That's why you need to check yourself frequently to become more aware when you're suffering from stress.

· Does your jaw ache?

· Do you frequently grind your teeth?

· Do you grip the steering wheel so tightly that your hands ache?

· Do you suffer from frequent headaches?

· Do you have periodic intestinal upsets?

· Do your muscles—especially those in the neck and shoulders—feel tight?

· Do you often feel your heart racing?

· Do you frequently find yourself angry at people?

· Is the expression, "I'm so irritated . . ." one you commonly use?

· Are you a perfectionist, with anything less making you feel like a failure?

· Do you suffer from a low self-esteem?

· Do you turn to eating, alcohol, or illegal drugs to help you relax?

· Do you frequently feel unappreciated and dumped on?

- Do you feel as though you have too many responsibilities?

- Are you always fatigued?

- Do you feel always rushed for time?

- Do you suffer from sexual dysfunction?

- Are you accident-prone?

- Do you hate to go to work in the morning or come home at night?

- Does someone in your immediate or extended family suffer from a chronic illness?

- Do you feel as though you have no control over your situation?

- Are you a chronic worrier?

The more "yes" answers you have to the questions above, the more stress you may be suffering. Become aware of your response to stress as well as what triggers stress in your life. Then you can alter those responses that can be changed and learn to relax with those that can't.

MAKE TIME TO RELAX

Don't laugh. Even with all you have to do, you can still make time to relax, to lift the stress from your aching shoulders, to finally be in control of your emotions. What's even more important, by your example you'll be passing this wisdom along to your spouse and to your children and stepchildren. By learning to cope with stress as a family, you may find that some of the problems you all had been struggling with have disappeared as well. What's more, by incorporating these relaxation techniques into your family traditions, you may have succeeded in drawing your family closer together.

• LEARNING TO RELAX •

Erase from your mind any thoughts about your not having time for yourself. If you don't take care of yourself first, you'll be in no shape to care for others. Unfortunately, there is no "Ten Ways to Help You Relax" list. What works for one may not help another. My niece once found it relaxing to jump out of perfectly safe airplanes while they're flying—with a parachute, of course. I used to get nervous on even a tall ladder. On the other hand, I find sailing relaxing, whereas someone who fears water would consider that stressful. Select what works for you and don't cause stress in others by insisting they do as you do. Allow them to discover what works best for them.

PROGRESSIVE RELAXATION

This form of relaxation has been around since the thirties, but many of us still haven't discovered it. In order to practice stress reduction, you must first isolate and then experience the sensation of being stressed. You may be walking around with a frown, tense jaw, tight neck and shoulder muscles and not even be aware of it.

There are two forms of progressive relaxation. The first is "active," called that because you first tighten a particular muscle group, then relax it, feeling the difference. Begin by shutting the door to your room or office so you won't be disturbed. Then get comfortable. Close your eyes and begin with the muscles in your forehead, first tightening, then relaxing them. Work on down throughout your chest, arms, hips, and thighs to your toes, curling your toes tightly, then relaxing them. You should feel a total sense of relaxation throughout your body.

With the second form, "passive relaxation," you also find a private place to sit or lie comfortably. Close your eyes and give mental messages to each muscle group, beginning with your forehead. Your thoughts should be along the lines of, "My forehead is relaxed. Very relaxed and warm. So relaxed." Continue with your cheeks and jaw, on down to your toes. As you move down your body, enjoy the warm and relaxed sensations you are feeling.

Practice either of these methods of progressive relaxation. The goal is the same: to create deep relaxation. Experts suggest doing progressive relaxation for ten to twenty minutes once or twice a day, but no more than that. "The idea is not to withdraw from the world," said one psychologist, "but to be equipped to handle stressful situations by being able to relax and release the tension you feel." Once you begin to feel comfortable with the process, you can call on it whenever needed throughout your day.

There are tapes that can help you if you find it difficult to think about what you're supposed to do next. But just as listening to a tape on perfecting your golf swing won't make you a Tiger Woods, you have to practice progressive relaxation. If you're diligent and don't expect to be an overnight success (and don't make yourself more stressed because you aren't perfect at it), you'll soon find yourself able to relax on cue, whether you're at the doctor's office, sitting in church or synagogue service, or at your desk. I often use it while I'm in the car, waiting for a light to change.

Although there are many books on relaxation, I'm partial to one of the first on the subject, *The Relaxation Response* by Herbert Benson, M.D., with Mariam Z. Kipper. Some books make relaxation techniques sound far more complicated than they really are. His doesn't.

When working with your children, it may help for you to sit quietly beside them, calling out instructions, such as: "Tighten your lips. That's it. Now relax. Let the warmth flow in. Good. Now your shoulders . . ." and so on. If your presence inhibits your youngsters, make an audiotape that they can slip into the tape player or write out a script and have them record it themselves.

MEDITATION

Many people still consider meditation to be some "new age" holdover from the 1960s. But it isn't. For centuries, native Americans, religious leaders, and performers and sports figures have used meditation to focus their minds and reduce stress.

It wasn't until 1968, when Dr. Herbert Benson of Harvard Medical School proved scientifically that meditation actually could reduce the physical effects of stress, that meditation was openly embraced by the medical world as a "real" way to reduce stress. Meditation offers a mental time-out from reality, filling you both physically and mentally with a sense of peace and tranquillity, thereby reducing stress.

Learning to meditate is fairly easy. As with the other forms of relaxation, you need to find a place where you won't be disturbed. That may be more difficult. But persevere. Get comfortable and close your eyes. Some people prefer to look at a flickering candle, so try it both ways. Let your mind go blank as you think of a relaxing scene, such as a gently flowing stream or a peaceful lake (unless you're afraid of water). Then focus on one word. It can be something that has spiritual meaning for you, such as "God," "Jesus," or "Buddha," or simply a word such as "one," "peace," or calm." When extraneous thoughts pop into your head (and they will), just let them float by and refocus on your word as you gently breathe in and out.

It takes a few sessions to get comfortable with meditation, but once you've mastered it, you'll find it can be used daily—while you're waiting in line, sitting in your office, doing the dishes, or waiting for a red light to change. Just keep your eyes open for the latter.

Years ago I heard a mother call her teenage son and ask, "Have you practiced your meditation yet?" At the time, I thought she was a little nutty. I now realize she was very wise as she prepared her youngster to handle stress throughout his life. Encourage your children/stepchildren to learn this important technique as well.

MASSAGE

Even people who swear they don't like to be touched are usually delighted to experience a professional massage from a licensed massage therapist. This "laying on of hands" has been used for relaxation and therapeutic purposes since ancient times in Greece and Rome and has been used in the Far East for centuries. Recently, many businesses are offering regular massage therapy to their employees.

Although there are many different styles of massage that differ depending on the type and amount of pressure applied, they all can help reduce stress. The kneading and stroking motions increases circulation, which is why you usually feel relaxed, yet energized after a treatment. Massage also removes toxins from your tissues, improves the immune systems, and helps you think more clearly. And yes, I have a weekly massage and can feel the difference when I miss a session.

You can find a qualified massage therapist at your health club or spa, by calling a local orthopedist or physical therapist or by contacting the physical education department of your local college or university. You also can call the American Massage Therapy Association's national office in Evanston, Illinois, at (847) 864-0123 and ask for the name of massage therapists in your area. Many massage therapists are willing to come to your home, but be sure to ask for references first. Some states require licensing before a massage therapist can work on clients. If your state is one of them, contact the Department of Professional Regulation, located in your state capital, to see if the massage therapist is licensed.

Your teenagers also might be interested in massage to reduce stress. If they're modest, they can keep shorts or briefs on, although they'll always be covered with a sheet except for the area being worked on. Massage therapy not only helps to reduce their stress, it also makes them aware of tension in their body so they can relax it before it begins to cause trouble.

BIOFEEDBACK

Biofeedback uses electronic monitoring instruments to give you information about your heart rate, brain waves, skin temperature, and muscle tension. By watching a video screen or hearing a hum or low beep, you can monitor your progress as you learn to slow or regulate your heartbeat, lower your blood pressure, or reduce muscle tension. This type of training is usually done with a psychologist or physician trained in the use of this type of monitoring device, although there are some devices sold commercially for personal use.

For more information on biofeedback, contact your local hospital or send a stamped, self-addressed envelope to: Biofeedback Society of America, 10200 West 44th Street, Suite 304, Wheat Ridge, Colorado 80033.

SELF-TALK

Never underestimate the importance of talking to yourself. It can help to reduce stress. You can become your own cheerleader, telling yourself, "Come on, you can do it. Relax . . ." When you feel the familiar signs of tension in your neck, tell yourself, "Relax. Calm. Let the tension float away." Many times, when I have felt rushed and frantic, I've told myself, "Slow down. Take it easy. Slow," and can feel the tension drift away.

You've probably used self-verbalization to help you work through everything from your golf swing, to gathering the ingredients to bake a cake, to assembling a child's toy on Christmas Eve, when you mumble, "Now the 'E' screw goes into the hole marked 'R,' while the 'S' peg . . ."

So you're really not learning a new technique with self-talk, but rather a new use for it. Talk yourself out of pyramid thinking, when you start piling one event that "might" happen onto another and another until you feel the entire stack of problems is going to teeter and topple over on you. Use self-talk to ease you through a stressful situation, such as talking to your ES, meeting with your kid's teacher, or giving a speech. Use self-talk the way Anna did in the hit musical, *The King and I*, when she sang, "Whistle a Happy Tune."

Another use for self-talk is called "thought stopping." Experts claim that seventy-five percent of what we think is negative. Since our bodies tend to react as our minds think, we can change the way we feel by stopping the negative thought and replacing it with one that is more positive. Tell yourself "stop," when you think, "I can't talk to these kids. I must have been crazy to get involved with their father," and instead say, "I'm making progress with these kids. They know I listen to them and that I care. Eventually we're going to be friends." Whenever you think, "I just can't do this," order a "stop" to such thinking, and replace the negative with a positive "Of course I can do this. I always have."

You also can use self-talk to reduce the stress created by anger or bitterness. Talk your way out of fights whenever possible. Don't get mad, get relaxed. Don't see red, see blue if it makes you think of a calm, peaceful river. Think green if it conjures up pictures of springtime with children laughing and baby lambs cavorting over a grassy meadow. When you feel angry, whisper your color code to yourself and let the picture it creates in your mind defuse your hostility and stress.

Pass these stress reduction techniques on to your children and stepchildren. Help them to really hear the negative comments they say aloud, and work together to change all comments—spoken aloud or to themselves—into positive self-talk. Help them to transform anger into the visualization of colors that create a sense of calming for them. It's a gift that will keep on giving for the rest of their lives.

VISUALIZATION

Researchers have proven that the pictures we create in our minds can affect our bodies and our reaction to stress. You can use your imagination to create visual images that will bring you a sense of calm and well-being.

Set aside a period where you can have time to develop your visualization powers. Close your eyes and breathe deeply three times, concentrating on your breath as it gently goes in, then out. Then try to visualize a place that gave you a sense of peace and tranquillity. It could be the beach, watching a beautiful sunset or sitting on the front porch of a cabin in the woods, listening to the rustle of autumn leaves and admiring their brilliant colors. My "safe place" exists only in my mind, but it's as real to me as any place I've ever been and it fills me with an amazing sense of calmness. I can see myself sitting on an old-fashioned swing on the top of a hill that overlooks a great harbor. There are sailboats just on the horizon. I can visualize myself swinging back and forth on that swing and almost feel the breeze against my cheeks. The salt air fills my lungs with every breath I take. As I slowly breathe in and out, I think "calm, calm," in time to the motion of the swing. It fills me with a great sense of peace and an "all's right in the world" feeling.

That exercise is another that you can share with your kids. They may surprise you with the "safe place" they select. As with the other relaxation techniques, you'll be teaching them a skill that will follow them into adulthood, helping them to cope with stress and making them feel more in control of their emotions. Visualization can be especially effective to help your kids feel less anxious when they go to their other home, especially if they feel uncomfortable or have difficulty coping with stepsiblings there.

EXERCISE

Our body's need for aerobic exercise has changed little since our cave-dwelling ancestors ran away to keep from approaching wild animals. Although times have changed, our nervous system hasn't. Exercise is the answer, not only playing an important part in keeping you physically fit, but in also protecting your emotional health. It is a real "stress buster." Exercise can become a family affair, with everyone involved in whatever the activity happens to be—jogging, walking, playing tennis, skiing, or swimming. It's also a good time to talk one-on-one to each of the kids as you walk or bike ride together.

Exercise also serves as an excellent time-out period when you feel you really need some time alone to regroup and can go running, biking, or work out at the gym to work off some tension. Be careful about becoming obsessive about exercise, though. You'll negate the benefits and create additional stress in your life.

ASSERTIVENESS TRAINING

One of the best things I ever did for myself to reduce stress was to take a course in assertiveness training. It does not teach you to become more aggressive. What assertiveness training does do is to teach you to stay in control by asserting yourself, rather than letting others manipulate you. While you may think that your parents do a pretty good job of manipulation, your kids and step-kids are the real experts.

The courses and books offering assertiveness training teach you that you have the right to feel a certain way without having to explain yourself and that you have the right to change your mind. You also learn that rather than getting in an argument with some-one, you can just state and then repeat what you want without going into further explanations. The latter is called the "broken record" technique and works well with kids. They quickly learn that whining and complaining doesn't move you. When you be-come more assertive, you learn how to say no and mean it.

You also learn to assert yourself about what *you* need to feel less stressed. You'll cut out activities you don't really enjoy or give yourself a time-out to do what the Romans did and take a relaxing bath. You'll take a day off to shop, see a museum exhibit, or browse at your favorite bookstore, or even become a volunteer. Many people have discovered a "helper's high" as they turn atten-tion from themselves and their problems and focus instead on someone else. Remember, too, that volunteer projects are also good activities for families. The kids learn about volunteering and the importance of helping others, while getting to know their bi-ological parent and stepparent in a different setting.

Obviously, there's a great deal more to assertiveness training, but it's an excellent technique to help reduce stress. Try it.

LAUGHTER

Laughter has a magical power to help reduce stress. It not only makes you feel good, but it's good for you as well. The late Nor-man Cousins is often credited with the recent acceptance, by lay and medical professionals alike, of the healing power of laughter. Laughing is the body's natural tranquilizer, as it brings additional air into your lungs and triggers the release of chemicals called endorphins, which help the body reduce stress. Laughter, what Cousins called "inner jogging," also helps to reduce blood pressure and muscle tension, improves circulation, and can even reduce pain and depression.

Find the humor in a situation and encourage your family to look for the funny side of the street. Just the words, "G-16" can make our kids giggle as they remember our driving over a bumpy road in California, only to discover that someone had inadvertently made a pencil mark on the map and that what we were following wasn't really an actual road that went anywhere. We ended up three hours late to our destination, but it's made a funny story over the years.

By developing a stronger sense of humor, you'll stop taking yourself so seriously. You'll also find that the family that laughs together is a happier family. It's a good way to blend two families together, too.

IMPROVE NUTRITION

Eating a balanced diet can help you and your entire family to reduce stress. Limit your fast food meals and spend some time at the library, bookstore, or on-line, reading about nutrition. If the kids are old enough, assign a "kid's day to cook," with the only requirement being that they plan a well-balanced meal. Then you offer to reward them by doing the clean-up.

GET ORGANIZED

There's no doubt that, for most of us, clutter and mess can cause stress. Unfortunately, stress may be intensified when you and your spouse disagree on just what constitutes clutter. Try to reach some agreement and hold a family meeting to describe the rules.

- Have specific places for things that tend to hide, such as glasses, car keys, and homework.

- Create a master calendar with room for everyone's activities. Mark the dates the stepchildren go to their other parent, so you won't have to keep asking.

- Have a grocery list for everyone to add what they "need." If it's not on the list, whoever does the shopping won't get it.
- Limit your collectibles so there's not so much to dust.
- Buy extras of things like lightbulbs, toilet paper, shaving cream, toothpaste, etc., so you don't have to make an extra trip for those items.
- Hang coat racks near the back door so everyone can hang coats, hats, baseball gloves, and scarves.
- Set priorities. You *can't* do it all yourself. Why try?
- Plan ahead.

ACCEPT THE IMPERFECT YOU

It's much less stressful when you accept that you aren't perfect. It's no sin. None of us are. But when you try to be the perfect spouse and the perfect stepparent, you are setting up unreachable goals. Be the best you can. Leave perfection to the angels.

ACCEPT AN IMPERFECT FAMILY

Sometimes this is more difficult than to accept an imperfect you. When you remarried, your dream may have been to have the perfect family. But you're setting yourself up for disappointment. The perfect family doesn't exist. Although we all have dreams for our kids, we can't control their lives or make them interested in (or good at) something just because we want them to be. It's much less stressful to be accepting of your kids and your spouse as well. Take them and love them, warts and all.

ANTICIPATE POTENTIALLY STRESSFUL SITUATIONS

There are some situations, such as life-cycle events and holiday time, that are stressful for most people. But they are particularly so for those in blended families. Holiday time, especially Christmas, is a reminder that the kids must be shared between their two biological parents, that the once fond memories of the familiar celebrations no longer can be realities. Finances may be strained as well.

Anticipate the emotions that will be felt during the holiday season and encourage your kids and stepkids to talk about them. Share your feelings as well. They may be surprised to learn that adults also feel torn and sad that things have changed. Acknowledge these changes and then plan for the future. Often the greatest stress arises in what is not said.

Practice some of the stress reduction techniques described in this chapter, especially during the holiday time. Lower your expectations about the holiday season. When you expect too much, you set yourself up for disappointment.

Prioritize your family's holiday activities so you don't try to make all the parties, bake cookies, shop, wrap gifts, and decorate the entire house, only to discover there's no time for your family to enjoy each other. Be sure everyone gets adequate rest. Watch your food and alcohol intake. Then work together as a blended family to create some meaningful new memories and traditions, creating joy among the bittersweet.

Once you learn to cope with stress, it loses its ability to harm you. Help your kids learn to recognize and cope with it, too, teaching that they remain in control of their emotions, rather than being ruled by them.

CHAPTER FOURTEEN

Twelve Ways to Trip with Steps

"The true way goes over a rope which is not stretched at any great height but is just above the ground. It seems more designed to make people stumble than to be walked upon."

—FRANZ KAFKA,
The Great Wall of China.
Reflections

*M*ost people go into a blended family situation desperately wanting to make it work. They've previously suffered from a relationship loss, either by divorce or death, and don't go easily into a new alliance, especially because children—theirs, the new spouse's, or both—are involved. But regardless of how hard they struggle with major issues, the men and women who have created and lived in blended families say it often is the little things that trip you up and lead to the big fallout. According to many experts, over half of all remarriages end in divorce.

Below are twelve ways in which people trip in stepfamilies. Become aware of these potential stumbling blocks so you can keep both your balance and your blended family intact.

1. Being impatient

Biological families are created slowly, with the couple having time to get used to themselves as a unit and each other's extended family before a child comes into the fold. In a blended family, however, two thirds of the family exists before the newcomer is admitted. The children have finally gotten used to being with one parent at a time since the divorce and don't welcome yet another change.

Suddenly, the new spouse and addition to the family pops up on the scene. It's like suddenly being the new boy or girl in the classroom or on the team. Everyone else knows the rules and group history but you. Too often the biological parent pushes the new spouse onto a fast track, expecting that the children will automatically fall in love with the stepparent just because he or she did. Just like two positive (or negative) fields of a magnet held together, the kids are repelled to the opposite direction immediately.

Sometimes it is the new stepparent who wants to "prove" that he or she is going to be a great addition to the family. The stepparent tries too hard for affection and approval, and by doing so, inadvertently pushes the kids away because they feel resentful and guilty about this person who is trying to supplant their mom or dad. The harder the stepparent tries to win the kids over, the more they resist. It's frustrating for the adult who only wants to reach out to the loved one's kids.

Remember to keep doing those things you did when you were dating their parent, such as bringing little gifts from time to time, occasionally slipping teens some gas money, or arranging some special time alone with the stepkids. Be patient. Love grows slowly, and it doesn't seem to matter if the stepchild is two or twenty.

"I was twenty-two when my mother remarried," a professional woman said. "My father had died a year ago. His two sons came to live with us too. I terribly resented them all coming into our home. It was ten years into their marriage before I finally accepted it.

"My stepfather tried to be kind and to be there for me. He even took me to a movie once without the other kids (my siblings and his kids) so we could get to know each other better. The movie was *Carnal Knowledge*. He thought it was "Cardinal," about Catholic priests. We left after the first five minutes and went out to dinner. But I rejected his attempts to get closer and fought to remain loyal to my father's memory. It wasn't until I was well into my thirties that I

realized how much I really liked him and how good he had been to
all of us. It made me sad to realize how much time and friendship I
had wasted."

When I asked her what her stepfather could have done differently, she answered:

*"I wasn't very nice to my mother and he tried to protect her.
I think it made things worse. He shouldn't have tried to take sides
and gotten into the middle of things. He should have encouraged
my mother and me to work things out without his involvement."*

2. Speaking without listening

Babies have it right. They do a lot of listening before they start
to babble. And they really don't start talking until they've listened
a great deal more. Somehow we adults have lost this ability, and
this lacking causes a lot of problems.

When you really listen to your stepkids without thinking about
what you're going to do next or how you will respond, you often
hear what they're *not* saying. Their hesitancy to bond with you
may be that they're afraid you'll leave them (or die), just like their
biological parent did. They may still be angry with their parents
for getting a divorce and their anger spills over to you just because
you're there. They also may be saying that you're moving too fast;
telling you to just put on a "friend face," as they're not ready to
accept another adult in a parenting mask just yet.

If you're the biological parent, you may be jumping in to tell
your new spouse to stop criticizing your kids, without listening to
discover that maybe they really do need a little tighter rein. You
may not hear your spouse's unspoken plead, "Let me be part of
the family, rather than a mute who stands by while your kids treat
you with disrespect."

Listen before you speak. That's a part of communication too.
For more detailed suggestions on how to create better communication in your blended family, turn to Chapter Three.

3. Having to always be right

You probably wouldn't go to a foreign country and begin to tell the natives what they're doing wrong. Yet many stepparents report that they feel a little like the Marines—needed to come in to clean up the mess.

> "My stepson was ten when I married his mother," a New England sports personality said. "He had been the man of the house since he was three. I had never had a child so I guess I came on a little too authoritative. My wife still tells me I can't give orders. My advice to others would be not to come on too strong. You have to understand that kids operate by a different set of rules. You have to change the way you listen and speak."

There is more than one way to do most things. Check out the landscape and see what your spouse has been accomplishing as a single parent. If you think yours is a better, faster, more economical, or simpler way, discuss it in private before you suggest it to the children.

> "It's different if you've never been a parent before," a thirty-three-year-old architect said. "You need to know something about parenting, developmental stages, and basically, how kids work. Coming in when your stepson is four is a little like opening a book in the middle of Chapter Four, not at the chapter on infancy. Healthy communication with your spouse helps a lot. My wife listens to my advice (even if she doesn't always take it). She thinks it's good to have a partner willing to find solutions. We really work well together."

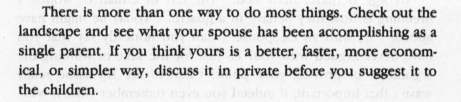

4. Staying angry or bitter

Staying angry or bitter at your ES (or your spouse's ex) is a good way to fall flat on your face in a blended family. Kids can read your expression and hear in your voice that you really hate their other biological parent. It makes them feel disloyal, guilty, and insecure, emotions most parents don't want their kids to feel.

These emotions also are not healthy for *you*, as they create additional stress, which raises your blood pressure, affects your digestive tract, triggers head and neck aches, and can also affect your immune system. While you don't have to actually like your ES, remember that your kids have his or her genes, too. Put the past behind you. Use exercise to rid yourself of the anger you've stored up. Anger can be harmful to your health and your kids' health as well.

5. Arguing for the sake of arguing

George Bernard Shaw said, "The test of a man or woman's breeding is how they behave in a quarrel." Today he might have added, ". . . with an ex-spouse." Can you honestly say that you have never argued with your ES just for the sake of winning the argument, of proving your point? Chances are the issue really wasn't that important, if indeed you even remember what it was.

Keep your discussions with your ES to the point, focused on what's best for your children. Any time the discussion moves off subject and perhaps onto an issue from your former marriage, pull it (dragging and screaming, if necessary) back to your central concern: your kids.

Still enjoy arguing? Join a debating society.

6. Making children the messengers

This is a massive no-no. You might as well play tug-of-war with the kids, substituting them as the rope. When you force your children to carry messages back and forth, you put them in a difficult and stressful position. They feel resentful at being used—which they are—and disloyal to one or both of you. (They also may mess up the message and quote you incorrectly.) What's more, when you make your kids your messenger, you also are empowering them to represent you. Are you really sure you want to do that?

If you really are miffed that the kids come to stay with you looking like characters from *Oliver Twist*, call Fagin (or Ms. Fagin) yourself and ask that the kids be returned in the clothes they were wearing when they went to "the other" house. Better yet, ask yourself if, in the real scheme of things, it is all that important. Just keep the good stuff at your house.

Don't have the kids ask the other spouse for money, either. If you haven't received your child support, that's an issue to be discussed by adults, not kids. If you need to put someone in the middle, make it your lawyer.

7. Using money as a power play

Using money as power play should be restricted for games of Monopoly only. Don't use it for punishment, such as telling your ES that he or she can't have the kids because the child support money is late. When you do that, you punish your kids, who may have been looking forward to seeing their other parent. You may turn out to be the bad guy.

If you're the stepparent, don't try to buy your stepchildren's favor by getting expensive gifts or paying for lessons in order to outshine your spouse's ES. The kids will probably see through your attempt, accept your expensive gifts, and then resent you for thinking they could be bought. Kids work in mysterious ways.

8. Forgetting that the children's well-being is your first priority

It's easy to get so caught up with "getting even" with your ES that your motive for most of your actions and decisions is revenge. Try changing this destructive attitude by using a technique known as "thought stopping." It involves changing your thoughts by consciously replacing them with a positive and healthier message. You can't hold two thoughts in your head simultaneously, so if you're thinking, "This discussion is for the good of my kids," you can't also be thinking, "This son-of-a-gun is going to tell me he can't pay for camp again," or worse, "She always makes me question my parenting skills."

Practice banning all violent or emotional language and substituting an objective approach. If necessary, repeat a calming mantra, such as "Avoid emotional traps." You may quickly discover that not only are your encounters with your ES less stressful, but that he or she also becomes less emotional and more objective during your meetings.

9. Neglecting your health

Just as football teams acknowledge an enthusiastic crowd as "the twelfth man," you and your spouse need to acknowledge the presence of the other biological parent as having an influence over your lives. Unfortunately, it may not always be a positive one. While you can control just how invasive the influence may become, it *is* there, and to deny that fact is not facing reality.

This added person in your lives often places extra stress on your new marriage, which can have harmful and often debilitating effects on your physical and emotional health. In addition, many remarriages involve two-career couples, which adds to the stress level. Be aware of these added pressures and take extra care to protect your health. This includes:

· maintaining a balanced diet

· making exercise a part of your lifestyle

· utilizing stress reducing techniques such as massage, relaxation exercises, yoga, biofeedback, meditation, and self-hypnosis

- avoiding known harmful activities, such as smoking, use of illegal drugs, excessive use of alcohol, and overexposure to the sun

- seeking therapy, if needed

- getting enough rest.

While you may laugh at the possibility of your ever getting enough rest, it is a vital and often overlooked part of reducing stress. What you can specifically do to reduce stress is discussed in greater detail in Chapter Thirteen.

10. Trying to take the place of the biological same-sex parent

Many new stepparents express a desire to bond immediately with the stepchildren. Unfortunately, it's probably a wish that is bound to be unfulfilled. As stated throughout this book, it takes time for real trust and love to develop and grow. Stepparents who have no children of their own seem to be the most inclined to jump right in. Those who do get bruised and their feelings hurt.

> "Although I would love to have my four-year-old stepson call me 'Daddy,' I wouldn't ask him to. I know he'd feel disloyal to his own dad doing that," said a stepfather of less than a year. "I try to stay open to his needs, not mine. I have different skills than his natural father, and share those with my stepson."

11. Forgetting to laugh

The English novelist, William Makepeace Thackeray, said "A good laugh is sunshine in a house." And so it is. Laughter reduces stress as it relaxes facial muscles and turns off the "fight or flight" response. It teaches children to laugh at themselves and take things in perspective, so they can learn from mistakes, rather than agonizing over them or becoming frozen for fear of repeating errors.

In her book, *The Male Stress Syndrome*, author Georgia Witkin, Ph.D., includes in her checklist of behaviors that may identify potential marital stresses, "I seem to have no sense of humor when I am at home."

That's not to say that there aren't problems in merging two families. There are. But laughter and the use of kind and gentle humor can help smooth over some of the rough spots. Make sure laughter finds a place in your blended family home.

12. Closing your heart to love

You may not realize that you have closed your heart to love. But the need for self-protection runs deep. You may be afraid to share your children with their stepparent because some hidden part of you fears the stability of your new marriage. "After all, if my first marriage failed . . ." you whisper in the secret part of your soul. So you protect yourself from vulnerability, not realizing that in giving and receiving love we must risk being vulnerable, must open our heart.

Those who are stepparents may deeply love their mate, but keep their heart closed to the stepchildren for the same reason: fear of failure. But the best way to bond with these children is to open your heart to them, and yes, to risk being rejected, to risk being hurt, and to risk losing them if your marriage fails. But oh . . . the benefits are grand.

HOW CAN YOU KEEP FROM TRIPPING?

You can keep from tripping by employing the same techniques you use when you find yourself in a strange hotel room and know you may need to get up in the middle of the night.

- · Take notice of your surroundings

- · Become aware of potential dangers

- · Remove obstacles so you won't trip over them

- · Use a night-light (otherwise known as love), to help you find your way.

CHAPTER FIFTEEN

Grandparents—the Great Equalizer

"Every generation revolts against its fathers and makes friends with its grandfathers."

—LEWIS MUMFORD: THE BROWN DECADES

*T*he late Dutchess of Windsor is credited with saying, "You can never be too rich or too thin." To this I'd like to add, "Or have too many grandparents." It doesn't really matter if they are biological grandparents or instant step-grandparents. What's important is that these individuals care about their grandchild and reach across the generations to bolster self-esteem and act as an impartial sounding board.

Grandparents are the great equalizer in a child's life; they are the strong safety in the "them versus us" game, which pairs grandparent and grandchild against the parent. Mindful of their own child-rearing errors (and acutely aware of those being made daily by their adult child), grandparents become a safe harbor when the sailing gets rough. It offers one that rarity in life—a second chance.

For most of us, grandparenting in itself is a two-way street of dreams. We not only receive wonderful hugs, sticky kisses, free-form pictures for our refrigerators, and gifts of wacky T-shirts and hats bearing our grandchildren's names, but we also get to enjoy the fun that comes with kids, usually without having to bear the responsibility for them. Our grandchild-rearing techniques may be from the Spock era (Dr. Spock, not *Star Trek*'s Mr. Spock), but for some odd reason, they tend to work better with our grandkids than they did with our kids.

To our own grown children, our role as grandparents often evokes a love/resentment relationship. Our kids usually love our being involved with *their* kids, but they often resent the fact that it seems so easy for us. They forget, somehow, that *we* are not sleep deprived and that we give their kids back to them when the little ones get fussy.

The grandparenting connection is likely to encounter bumpy waters, however, when our adult child gets divorced. Often, their ES wants to toss us out along with our kid and pretend we don't exist. But that's a lose-lose situation for everyone involved.

▪ YOUR EX-SPOUSE'S PARENTS ARE *STILL* ▪ YOUR CHILDREN'S GRANDPARENTS

After a bitter divorce, it's natural to want to shed all traces of the marriage—the wedding pictures, love letters, the wedding band, along with your ES's immediate family, especially, so it often seems, your mother-in-law. But when you have children from the marriage, the grandparent ties will never be completely severed. In your haste to dump as much baggage as you can, don't toss out the ties to your ES's parents. Not only do they remain your children's grandparents, but they also can be supportive of both you and the children and serve a vital function as grandparents, even when you remarry.

Many divorced parents, even those with sole custody of a child, remain close to their ex's parents because they recognize the love and support (emotional as well as financial) emanating from that generation.

"David's parents always were supportive of me," recalled Meg, who had divorced her children's father when the youngsters were just two and three. "It was no secret that David drank and ran around. While they loved him—after all, he was their son—they also understood that it was an unhealthy situation for me and for their grandchildren. They helped with the baby-sitting chores so I could go back to school to get my degree and often took the kids clothes shopping when they suspected that David hadn't come through with any child support. Unfortunately,

they both died when the kids were in their early teens so my ex in-laws
never saw them as the responsible adults they grew to be. But I'll always
be grateful to them for being supportive to me as well as the children."

▪ SHOW THAT YOU WANT A CONTINUED RELATIONSHIP ▪

WHEN YOU'RE THE PARENT, NOT THE GRANDPARENT

Your former parents-in-law may feel self-conscious when their
adult child's marriage breaks up. Although parents know (even if
they don't always acknowledge) their own child's failings, your ex
is still their child and they have the need to be supportive of their
own. At some level, they may feel it's disloyal to remain friendly
to you, even though you may have enjoyed a close relationship for
all the years of your marriage. On the other hand, these former in-
laws, your children's grandparents, may feel awkward about reaching out to you or even calling for fear you might reject them. Yet,
they want to stay close to their grandchildren, so they're really
torn.

Don't shut out your children's grandparents unless there's an
extremely good reason (such as sexual or physical abuse) to do so.
Help bridge this troubled period by calling them yourself. After all,
you're younger than they are and hopefully, more flexible. Ask if
they'd like to take the kids out for lunch by themselves or come
to the park with you all for a picnic. If your children are in school
or extracurricular activities, encourage the grandparents to come
to the softball game or school play. If they refuse, don't give up.
Send notes about school activities and have the children send papers from school. Continue to maintain contact and let them know
that you understand that they have grandparent rights, even if you
and their adult child are no longer married.

When you're remarrying, give them time to get to know the
person who will be with you, helping to raise their grandchildren.

Although your former in-laws want you to be happy and go on with your life, they may have difficulty accepting "some stranger" as a stepparent to their grandchildren. Understand this and be patient.

Don't expect your own parents to move quickly in accepting your new marriage partner either. They may still feel close to your ES, and even though they understand your reasons for the divorce, they could miss the former relationship, especially if it was built up over many years during your marriage. Your parents really don't know this new spouse and may worry about whether or not he or she will be good to you and your children. They may wonder if their contact with their grandchildren will change. In case you haven't noticed, even parents of adult kids worry. It must be due to some hormonal change that occurs once you become parents and is a permanent condition.

It's important for you to talk to your new spouse about your previous relationship with your parents and describe what they have been like as grandparents. Your children's stepparent may bring into the marriage a history that affects what he or she considers to be the "proper" grandparenting role. This image of grandparenting could be far different from what your parents have been projecting since the time you first announced you were pregnant. It may be very difficult for them to change, if indeed, you really want them to. If you like the way they have grandparented in the past and your new spouse considers it too "hands on" or "too distant," you need to work out a compromise.

Nancy Wasserman Cocola writes in her book, *Six in the Bed*, "It is important for couples to have a realistic expectation of how change can and will occur with their parents. Expecting things to change less and more slowly than you might wish is probably an excellent idea. If a couple enters these dialogues with their parents knowing that actual change will probably fall short of their ideal, it leaves them free of the weight of disappointment."[1]

[1]Cocola, Nancy Wasserman, *Six in the Bed: Dealing with Parents, In-Laws and Their Impact on Your Marriage* (New York, 1997), pp. 173, A Perigee Book, Published by Berkley Publishing Group.

▪ WHAT SHOULD PARENTS DO IF THE GRANDPARENTS ▪ STILL MAINTAIN AN ARMED CAMP?

Some grandparents continue the war long after the divorced parents have made their peace, however uneasy, with one another. If you have sole custody, you may hesitate to let your kids spend a day with your ex's parents, knowing that the kids will hear how the divorce was all your fault, that you run a sloppy house, or that you're stingy with money. If you can still communicate with your former in-laws face-to-face, advise them that although you're happy for them to see their grandchildren, it upsets the children to hear unpleasant things about their mother/father. If it troubles you to speak directly to them, write them a note or speak to them on the phone. In the long run, a face-to-face meeting, however stressful, is usually more satisfactory because there tends to be less misunderstanding.

If your former in-laws rebuff any of your attempts to communicate your desire for a "truce" when it comes to the kids, just remind the children that Nana and Grandpa are still upset about the divorce and may say things that hurt your feelings. Forewarning them before the visit is better than waiting until the children come home in tears or worse, in silence.

WHEN YOU'RE THE GRANDPARENT

If you're the grandparent whose son or daughter does not have custody, make every effort to stay in touch with your grandchildren, even if you have to deal with "that person." You may be the one constant in your grandchildren's lives, proof to the confused youngsters that some relationships do last. You also serve as an important source of loving and caring.

Grandparents are, and always have been, the bearers and transmitters of memories. You are the storytellers, letting the children know that their parents also had scary times and fought the fear; that they also failed, but came back to other successes; and that they also did really dumb things at times when they were kids (and still do, in your mind, but you don't have to share that information). This contact between the generations is important on two levels; it reaffirms the vitality of "old age," counteracting stereotype information your grandchildren may otherwise receive from the media about "old people," and it strengthens their sense of security and continuity, something your grandchildren sorely need at this point. Your adult child may have divorced his or her spouse, but no one divorced the offspring.

If there is anger on the part of your former daughter or son-in-law and you're told that you can't see your grandchild, try to discuss the issue without being emotional. Explain—in person, if possible, but in writing or over the phone if necessary—that you understand but regret the bitterness between the former marital partners, and in the interest of your grandchildren, you want to continue to maintain the grandparent-grandchild relationship. Agree to set ground rules and resolve to stick to them. These should include:

1. Neither you nor your child's ES with custody will speak ill of the other or the noncustodial ES to the child.

2. You agree to discuss any major purchases for your grandchildren with the custodial parent *before* making them and before telling your grandchildren about them.

3. You will pick up the child at a set time and specific location agreed upon by both you and the custodial parent.

4. You will return the child at a set time and specific location agreed upon by the two of you.

What if, despite all your best efforts, the child's custodial parents refuses to let you have visitation rights? Then you must learn what rights you have and enforce them.

WHAT ARE THE GRANDPARENT'S RIGHTS?

Grandparents rights vary greatly from state to state, but in most states, grandparents can go to the courts to petition for visitation rights. For specific information concerning your particular state's regulations, check with your community's social services or child advocacy division. You also can write to: Grandparents United for Children's Rights, Inc., 137 Larkin Street, Madison, Wisconsin 53705.

■ WHEN YOU BECOME INSTANT STEP-GRANTPARENTS ■

You probably suspected that there was a good chance that you were about to become a step-grandparent when your son or daughter became seriously involved with someone who had a child. However, the reality may really not set in until after the wedding. "Real" grandparents have six or seven months to adjust to becoming grandparents—as soon as they are told about the blessed event-to-be. That's enough time for most to knit a baby blanket, buy the crib, or whatever else they want to do to celebrate the anticipated grandchild and their entree to immortality. Your waiting period usually is far less when you become a step-grandparent—and the "baby" may be six, ten, or fourteen, far too old for a blanket or crib.

You also may have only met your future step-grandchild a few times and frankly (as you told your hairdresser or bowling buddy), you didn't like the kid so much. He or she was whiny, hyperactive, and plain spoiled. You worry about what your adult child is getting into and you're not real sure how to act toward this new kid on your block. Besides, you've got two "real" grandchildren. Where does this new stepgrandchild fit in?

YOU DON'T HAVE TO LOVE YOUR STEP-GRANDCHILDREN

It's often a relief for instant step-grandparents to know that they don't have to love their step-grandchildren. Love isn't an instant emotion, available upon demand; it takes time to grow. The fact is, you may never really feel as though you truly love this grandchild by remarriage; on the other hand, over the years you may develop a respect and fondness, and yes, even a love for the youngster.

"After four years, my parents still are reserved with my stepson," a television personality said with some sadness. "I've told them I'd like them to show more affection, but I can't make them. They are crazy for our new baby, but they just can't seem to share some of that love with my stepson. They're not mean to him or anything, but it's obvious that they don't think of him as a true grandson."

WHAT TO CALL STEP-GRANDPARENTS AND STEP-GRANDCHILDREN?

It's really a no-win situation here. You feel as though you're treading water and don't know which (if either) shore offers a haven. Some step-grandparents have introduced themselves to others as the youngster's grandparent, only to be corrected in no uncertain terms by the child that they aren't grandparents, but step-grandparents.

When I knew I was going to be a step-grandmother, I decided not to agonize over the decision, but to go to the expert. I asked my daughter-in-law what she wanted me to call myself, "step-grandmother" or "grandmother." She said the latter, if I was comfortable with it, which I was and am. Although I refer to myself as my step-grandson's grandmother, I have "friends" who hasten to correct me with, "You're only his step-grandmother, not his grandmother." For some reason, they had more of a problem with it than I did.

It surprised me to discover that their discomfort with terminology was contagious. One day, when I went to pick Joshua up from school, I identified myself by name and said I was there to pick him up. The teacher's aide asked what my relationship to him was. "I'm Joshua's grand . . . step . . . ," I stammered, finally blurting out, "I'm his stepfather's mother," which really confused her for a second or two. There ought to be a better name. And there is. I'm "Grammy."

Rather than worrying about what to call yourself, ask your new daughter or son-in-law, or if the kids are old enough, ask them.

Tell the youngsters if you have a specific preference as to what you want to be called and ask if that's a comfortable fit. If your step-grandchildren call their other grandparents "Grandpa John and Grandma Mary," they might prefer to use your first names the same way. If you have other grandchildren, you might want to suggest the name that's used by the other grandchildren, assuming the child isn't already using that name for another existing grand-parent. If other grandparents are "Nana" or "Poppie," and you ask to be called that as well, it not only will be confusing, but it also may make them feel disloyal.

Fortunately, kids never seem to struggle with what to call grandparents. It's obviously easier (and less emotional) than nam-ing a new stepparent and often is far more creative as well. Some of the grandparent appellations were discussed in Chapter Two, but others are equally unique. Grandchildren of John and Sue Wilke of Pittsville, Wisconsin, come to visit their grandparents on the family farm. What do they call them? "Grandpa and Grandma Moo." United States Senator Bob Graham and his wife, Adele, have nine grandchildren, all of whom call them "Doodle" and "Dee-dle." My own kids called my mother "Pool Nanny" (because she had a swimming pool) and my husband's mother "No Pool Nanny," because she didn't. A little materialistic, perhaps, but it helped to distinguish between the two grandmothers.

INSTANT GRANDPARENTING REQUIRES FLEXIBILITY

Becoming a grandparent certainly is one of life's great events. With the joy, however, come a few changes in lifestyle. Once your own kids were grown, you may have moved into a smaller house, condo, or apartment. You may travel more or spend more time on hobbies of one sort or another. You may finally have installed the white carpeting you always yearned for. Then grandchildren ap-pear on the scene.

Suddenly, your "second honeymoon cottage" seems too small for the crib, highchair, and playpen you need when the grandbaby comes to visit. You change or cancel altogether trips that were planned; your white carpeting gets stained with grape juice; you put away the china and crystal knickknacks. If something gets broken, you're upset, of course, but after all, they're your son or daughter's children and "kids will be kids."

When the grandchildren are "someone else's kids," (i.e., your adult child's spouse), it might be more difficult to be so agreeable. You may become resentful if the kids' noise prevents you from enjoying your favorite football game, or if they accidentally rip your great-grandmother's lace tablecloth with a fork, or when they play tag inside and bump into your antique end table, spilling your Limoges china collection on the floor and breaking some of the pieces. On the other hand, my guess is it could bother you just as much if they were your biological grandchildren.

Remember, too, that child-rearing theories change over the years. What was good enough for your kids is probably history today. Don't blame it on the new spouse. Chances are your own adult kid thinks that way too. If asked to baby-sit your step-grandchild, bite your tongue and don't argue when your daughter or new daughter-in-law tells you that the baby must sleep on its back, not its tummy. (It seems to lower the incidence of Sudden Infant Death Syndrome, known as "S.I.D.S."). Just smile when you're told to give the baby a cold bottle, rather than warming it. Don't act surprised to learn that spankings have given way to "time-outs," and "Because I said so" has succumbed to trying to reason with the kid.

It also doesn't matter that your own adult child may have done differently raising his or her kids in the first marriage. This present marriage is the one that exists today, and the one that you must support. Kids are resilient, so it really doesn't matter on this really rather minor stuff. Go along with it, just as *your* parents did (or you wished they had done) when you determined to raise your kids the "modern" way. Stepfamilies are under a great deal of stress just by virtue of trying to blend two families into a cohesive unit. Don't add to their stress level. Your adult child and the new spouse need your support and respect.

WHAT IF YOU AREN'T REALLY A "KID" PERSON?

Even if you really aren't a "kid" person and you didn't have the opportunity to get used to seeing these children as babies and watching them grow, you can learn to adjust to your instant status as a step-grandparent. Go with the positives that come with instant grandchildren:

- You don't have to wait for them to grow out of infancy to interact with them. Even toddlers are more responsive to your attentions than a newborn.

- You can begin with activities that bring you together and offer a minimum of talk if you are at a loss for words, such as movies, plays, computer games, athletic events, sailing, and fishing. Don't be surprised, however, if these events serve as a bridge between the generations and you find pleasure in seeing your new grandchild enjoying activities that you relish. It's hard to be ill at ease when you're helping your ten-year-old step-granddaughter take her first fish off the hook and put it on the stringer or when you're cheering at a football game with your new step-grandson.

- Listen. That's it. Just listen. In this busy world, a youngster's parents and stepparents often don't have (or make) the time for good old-fashioned one-on-one listening. If your new step-grandchild knows that you're ready and willing to hear his or her opinion, fears, or just general comments, you may turn on the communicating machine. I well remember late nights sitting up talking with my grandmother, hearing her tell how my grandfather courted her with a buggy drawn by two beautiful black horses and that she didn't know until they were married that one was borrowed. She *was* my biological grandmother, but she didn't have to be. Her stories of living history were fascinating. So would your tales of manual typewriters, ice boxes, telephone operators that said, "Number please," and life before television, microwaves, cell phones, and computers.

As a step-grandparent, you have a wonderful opportunity to make a strong impact on your grandchildren. Try to be a participatory grandparent, rather than a shadowy figure known only for sending a card or check for birthdays and Christmas or Hanukkah. Tell the kids about their stepparent's background and family history, which may be different (and therefore interesting) from their biological parents. Invite them over to make ice cream sundaes, decorate cookies, or to take part in a formal tea party, with your best china and silver. (My grandson was fascinated with the sugar cubes and tongs. To him, the tea was secondary.) It's a wonderful opportunity to sneak in some subtle and painless training on etiquette and manners, while having a good time, too.

Share some of your skills with these instant grandchildren. Teach them how to cook, needlepoint, repair things around the house, do magic tricks, or play chess. Take them with you when you go to cast your ballot at election time, deliver Meals on Wheels, or go grocery shopping. Do them the honor of just listening when they tell about their dreams, their fears, and their ideas.

You may not remember what it was like when you were parenting, but there were so many responsibilities that it often was hard to make time to just listen to your kids. Grandparenting gives you that precious second chance. I used to laugh when my father would get down on the floor so he could look eye-to-eye with my toddler son. But he was right (as I now realize he often was). He was paying my child the greatest compliment an adult can give to a kid—his undivided attention.

If your new grandchildren are adolescents, it might take them a little longer to accept you as a "real" grandparent. Be patient. Don't just ask, "How's school?" but take the time to learn the names of their teachers, what courses are their favorites, and which ones they hate. Without boring them with tales of, "When I was your age . . ." do share stories of times that you failed at something, when you were afraid, or when you felt insecure. These are emotions most young people can easily identify with. It may be comforting for them to know that you had some of the same feelings that they now struggle with and that you survived them.

One of the delights of being an instant grandmother to slightly older kids is that you can play "Auntie Mame" with them, by taking them shopping to the mall or flea market, to the theater or sporting event, and even on an out-of-town day or overnight trip. The kids probably will be flattered by your attention and excited by the new experiences. You'll enjoy their fresh outlook on things. It not only is fun for you, but it also gives their parents a nice break from parenting.

MAKE YOUR HOME SAFE FOR INSTANT GRANDCHILDREN

When you have biological grandchildren, you begin (or should begin) to check your home environment to make sure it's safe for them even before the kids begin to crawl. But when you suddenly are confronted with a two-year-old or a four-year-old step-grandchild, it may not occur to you to do a safety check. It may have been years since your other grandchildren were small, and when you haven't been around little ones for a while, you tend to forget how quickly they can get into things.

In order to illustrate my newspaper article, "How to Avoid Poisoning Your Child," (based on my own two-year-old daughter getting into the baby aspirin, which had been placed on top of a tall dresser), I used my youngest child, then age one, as a model for the photographer. We put cleaning supplies under the sink and placed the baby on the floor across the kitchen from the sink. I turned to say something to the photographer. In that fraction of a second, my son crawled across the floor and was about to pick up an open can of cleanser. I had forgotten how fast a baby could crawl.

Your purse may be the most dangerous threat to children, especially during the holidays. "Accidental poisonings are the main holiday-related emergency we see," said Dr. Marcus J. Hanfling, director of the Pediatric Injury Center at Baylor College of Medicine in Houston. "In all the hubbub of family visits, medications often are left out or within easy reach of children."

If you keep pills in your purse, keep your handbag on a top shelf in a closet, away from a toddler's inquisitive hands. Remove bottles of medication from your end table or bedroom night table as well. Prescription drugs are not the only hazard. Laxatives, iron pills, aspirin, vitamins, antihistamines, and some paints used for decorating model planes and other hobbies are all potentially poisonous as well.

Here are just a few additional suggestions to help you child-proof your home:

- Remove cleaning supplies from under your sink and put them on a higher shelf.

- Turn the handles of saucepans toward the back of the stove so toddlers can't reach up and spill the hot contents on themselves.

- Put safety protector plugs in your unused electrical outlets.

- Move sharp knives and scissors out of a youngster's reach. Remember, even a toddler can pull a chair over to a counter and climb up.

- Unplug appliance cords so they don't dangle over your countertops.

- NEVER leave a young child alone in the bathtub.

- Never put a crib or highchair near looped window cords.

- Keep plastic bags, especially those that come from the dry cleaners, away from young children.

- Remove scatter rugs that can slip and trigger a fall.

- Install a gate if you have stairs in the house.

- Remove or lock up any guns in the house.

- Learn CPR.

- Keep the number of your nearest Poison Control Center by every telephone.

According to James Lynch, MD, director of the Benedumn Pediatric Trauma Program, Children's Hospital of Pittsburgh, the best thing you can do to childproof your home is to get down on your hands and knees and crawl around. "You can see what a child sees down there. Kids explore with their hands and mouths," Lynch explains. "Buy drawer locks and install them on dressers and cabinets. Tape down loose cords, and throw away any frayed cords immediately."

There are other dangers in a home that are less obvious. According to Lynch, "Each year at least forty kids drown in toilets and five-gallon buckets. Parents and grandparents should buy toilet lid locks to prevent accidental drowning and remove five-gallon buckets from the house completely."

If you drag your adult child's old crib down from the attic for your step-grandchild, be sure that the slats aren't too wide. Older cribs usually don't meet present standards regulations. If the slats are too far apart, a child can slide through and be strangled. If you live in an apartment or high-rise condo, be sure that the windows have locks on them. If you have sliding doors that lead to balconies, install safety locks on them as well.

If you have pets, remember that your animals may not be used to children. Never leave your step-grandchildren alone with a pet, until you and the parents are confident that the children will not frighten or hurt your pet and that the pet is comfortable with children. Unfortunately, some older pets never reach that stage.

This information is not meant to frighten or overwhelm you, but only to make you more aware of the potential dangers we all have in our homes. The best way to prevent accidents is to be knowledgeable about what causes them.

■ PARENTS ARE OFTEN THE CAUSE OF DIFFICULTIES ■
BETWEEN CHILDREN AND STEP-GRANDPARENTS

When there are problems that exist between children and their step-grandparents, they often evolve not from that relationship, but rather because of the expectations of the parents.

"The main thing I see in my adult stepchildren is that they seem to be looking for a relationship with their perceived image of a father, rather than getting to know the living man," a stepmother said. "Their perception of how my husband and I should be as grandparents also doesn't take into account the reality of our lives. These seven grandchildren were only brought into our lives two years ago. Prior to that, we didn't really know of their existence, a choice made by my stepsons, I might add. They have always known where we were, but not so in reverse . . . My husband and I do the grandparent thing in remembering birthdays, buying gifts, cards for things like Halloween, and so on . . . My stepsons' fantasy grandparents take children on outings, overnight stays, and such. I'm in a wheelchair and have physical limitations so outings are difficult. Our townhouse is too small for company . . . I believe the one factor that prevents my stepchildren from having a mutually satisfying relationship with their father is that they are so busy chasing their perceived image of 'father' and 'grandfather' that they totally miss the experience of getting to know the reality of who and what their father actually is. This sets the relationship up for failure in that neither my husband nor I can realistically meet their expectations. And each time we fail, the shadows of estrangement loom larger."

Grandparents are, of course, as different as people are individualistic. One grandparent may believe "children should be seen and not heard." Another may squat on the floor and play "Candyland" with the grandkids. One may plan elaborate Halloween parties for the grandchildren, while another may just prefer sitting quietly and reading to them. Just as we may have wished for parents who were "more supportive," "more loving," or "more anything else," grandparents may not always fit our fantasy of what we'd like them to be. If we, as parents, can step back and let the grandparents interact with their grandchildren—instant and otherwise—in their own way, we may be surprised with the results.

Some grandparents may really feel uncomfortable interacting with children, especially stepchildren with whom they have no history and feel they have nothing to talk about. But, if left to their own devices, they may become most ingenious in bridging the generations. A grandmother may show the kids how to knit, work with clay, or re-pot plants as her relationship with her instant grandkids flourishes. A granddad may allow the kids into his basement workshop and actually let one of them pound a few nails with his favorite hammer. Before you know it, they may start building a boat together, as they build a stronger relationship as well.

▪ GRANDCHILDREN—STEP OR BIOLOGICAL— ▪ LET YOU BE A CHILD AGAIN

One of the things I like best about being a (step) grandmother to Joshua is that it gives me permission to enjoy my second childhood. Thanks to him I've gotten to see movies I otherwise wouldn't have, like *The Lion King* (I cried), *The Little Mermaid* (I cried), and *Aladdin* (I laughed). I buy all the Disney tapes and can't wait to see them with him. He gave me the excuse I felt I needed to visit the wonderful Children's Museum in Portland, Maine, and to go to the petting farm where he, his grandfather, and I saw our first live llama. (I think we were more impressed than he was.) We've gone to the big downtown library, where I helped him get his very own library card and to the Florida Aquarium, where we both were fascinated seeing that the "playful otters" really do play.

With him I bake and decorate sugar and oatmeal cookies (without raisins). For him I check the grocery store looking for "connect the dot" books, which, at age five, he devours. I've unpacked the boxes of my own children's favorite toys and books that I had saved and love watching Joshua enjoy real wood and metal trucks, instead of the plastic ones he's used to. He plays with his stepdad's original *Star Wars* figures. I understand they may be worth a great deal of money today, but I'm getting far more value watching a new generation enjoying them.

All this didn't happen the instant my husband and I met our step-grandson-to-be. It gradually developed over about a year's time. The hardiest relationships, like plants, take time and care to grow. Don't worry if you, as a step-grandparent, don't "have fun" the first time you're together with the step-grandchild. Go slowly and don't overwhelm the child with your attentions or yourself with your expectations. Be yourself, not some fantasy of how you think you should act, and be honest if you really don't feel up to some one-on-one time just now. Kids are very intuitive; they know when you're faking. Give yourself time to get used to the idea of becoming an instant grandparent.

WHAT IF YOU HAVE BIOLOGICAL GRANDCHILDREN AS WELL?

In addition to Joshua, I have an adorable biological grandchild, a little girl. She's not yet two and doesn't live in town, so there's not a great deal of interaction between them yet, although he seems fascinated just watching her while she looks up at him and laughs. Because of their difference in ages and the geographic logistics, I haven't gotten them together much, but as they get older, it will be fun to include her in our "Grammy days."

If you have other grandchildren, don't feel as though you have to entertain casts of thousands at one time. Actually, it's often nice (for you and the grandchild as well) to have just one kid at a time, regardless if they're biological or step. But do spread out your attentions and try to be fair. Kids keep score and will know if you obviously favor some over others. While gifts don't need to be all the same or even cost the same, try to keep them within a similar range. Never give large amounts of money or expensive gifts to your grandchildren without asking your adult child and his or her spouse for permission. They may have refused to buy a new bike for your step-grandson because he showed no responsibility for the two he lost. They won't appreciate your largesse, no matter how well meaning you are.

"I give my grandchildren money for Christmas and their birthdays," a seventy-plus year-old grandmother confided. "When my son remarried and I had two instant step-grandchildren, I gave them the same amount as the others. I treat them all the same and love them. I consider myself lucky to have so many wonderful young people who seem to want to spend time with me."

• OVER THE RIVER . . . TO WHOSE HOUSE? •

Holiday time can be a nightmare for blended families with extra grandparents and other relatives, not to mention scheduling stepchildren's celebrations with their other parent. It's not uncommon for kids to have three or four sets of grandparents after divorce and remarriage. While that means a lot of loving heading their way, it also presents a potential problem when *all* the grandmothers want the kids for dinner at Thanksgiving, and Christmas or Hanukkah. Hanukkah, of course, carries an easy solution because it is celebrated for eight days, enough for each set of grandparents to have a turn and still have days leftover for the parents to enjoy. Christmas and Thanksgiving present more of a problem, since there's a limit to how many turkey dinners one little person can eat and how many gifts he or she can open before becoming glassy-eyed.

"Holidays became a terrible strain," a mother of an eight-year-old boy, a six-year-old stepson, and an eleven-month-old infant said. "The scheduling at Christmas so my stepson could spend some time at his mother's house and my son to go to his father's when it was his turn became so confusing that we decided to alternate years. That meant one year we'd only have *our* child, but on alternating years we'd have our entire family. Then my husband's parents and mine couldn't agree whose house we'd go to, so we ended up hosting both sets of grandparents this year. The effort to cook for everyone seemed minor to the squabbling we'd had before."

Take some of the pressure off your adult child and his or her spouse by offering a Thanksgiving brunch celebration the Sunday before Thanksgiving or an early Christmas dinner or luncheon. Invite the family over for Boxing Day, celebrated in Great Britain, New Zealand, Canada, and Australia on December 26. Take the fourth or fifth night of Hanukkah and make it new and special for your family tradition. "But we've always done it that way" must give way to compromise. Often, you'll find that your new tradition is more relaxed and more fun than cramming an already busy day with more activities and food, leaving everyone exhausted and irritable.

▪ WHAT TO DO WHEN A NEW BABY COMES ▪

You've made your peace with your new son- or daughter-in-law and enjoy his or her children, accepting them as your grandchildren—to heck with the "step" business. Then you're told the good news: There's going to be a new baby. A "real" grandchild. What should you do to keep from upsetting the comforting status quo that's been established?

1. Don't refer to the new baby as your "real" grandchild. The others are not "pretend" ones.

2. If you think your adult child is crazy to have wanted another child at this point in his or her life, keep your opinion to yourself. It's none of your business.

3. If the baby has your adult child's forehead, nose, or eyes and you feel compelled to comment, remind your step-grandchildren how they resemble their biological parents as well. You may find, however, that your step-grandchildren have also picked up a few of your adult child's mannerisms, especially if they were young when your child came into their lives.

4. When you bring gifts for the baby, bring a little something for the other grandchildren as well. If some of them are in their teens,

bring gift certificates for movies or tapes, telephone cards, or
I.O.U's for a lunch or dinner with just the two of you.

5. Spend some time one-on-one with your step-grandchildren
away from the new baby, reminding them that babies are "too
little" to go to the zoo, movies, or shopping. The older kids need
to be reassured by your attention more at this point than the infant
does.

6. If you feel you can't be impartial, see the children separately.
Little children (as well as big ones) have feelings, too; don't hurt
them.

Unfortunately, because of the deadline for this book I've had
to rely strictly on others for the above information concerning new
babies. My son and daughter-in-law (Joshua's mother) are expecting a baby in April, after this manuscript in due at the publishers.
However, I plan to follow this advice.

CHAPTER SIXTEEN

Twelve Secrets for Successful Stepparenting

"Parenthood remains the greatest single preserve of the amateur."

—ALVIN TOFFLER,
Author of *Future Shock*

*P*arenting and stepparenting is probably the most challenging job you can tackle, yet there are no job requirements (other than having kids). It doesn't require getting a child care license, serving an apprenticeship, passing an exam, or getting a degree. Worst of all, no instruction manual comes with the kids. You certainly wouldn't buy a refrigerator or computer that came with so little back-up information.

That's why this chapter quote rings true. You're *not* professional parents, you're amateurs. What's more, even the professional counselors and therapists you go to for advice struggle just as much on a personal basis with their kids because it's hard to stand away and be objective about your own.

So relax. Trust your instincts. Follow the advice of the American physician and author, Benjamin McLane Spock. He wrote, "The more people have studied different methods of bringing up children, the more they have come to the conclusion that what good mothers and fathers instinctively feel like doing for their babies is usually best after all."

This advice was echoed by a Tampa pediatrician, Lane France, who said, "The biggest problem I see with young parents today is that they don't trust their own judgment." Parents and stepparents interviewed for this book agreed with this counsel and happily divulged their secrets for success in blending their families.

1. Communicate

This was the number one suggestion on everyone's list. Communication, which includes listening as well as speaking, is the key to opening the door to conflict resolution, for creating better understanding, and for solving problems that are bound to come up in daily life. Stepfamilies may have some difficulty with communication skills in the beginning. That's because the family members come from different original families, bringing with them varying styles of communication, different jargon, and dissimilar body language. But with time, patience, and practice, they should begin to blend even their communication styles and meet with success.

Open communication helps to keep expectations realistic.

> "It startled me to realize that my new husband loved his own kids as much as I did mine," a newly remarried woman told me. "I guess that should have been obvious. But I wanted him to instantly love my girls as I did. When we started talking about it, I understood why he couldn't. It wasn't just a question of loyalty. He didn't have the history with my kids. We both knew we'd have to take things more slowly. I'm glad we could talk about it."

2. Be flexible

The happiest and least stressed stepfamilies seem to be those in which all the members are flexible and willing to compromise when necessary. This includes being willing to change plans when needed. With so many individuals in their lives—including the other biological parent, stepsiblings, half siblings, and extended family—schedules often don't adhere to a rigid timetable. While routine is important, especially for younger children, the ability to adapt creates a less stressful environment for everyone. It's a good idea for all of us.

Realize too that a "bonus baby" coming into the family will change your lives once again. Fortunately, most blended families said the changes created by the arrival of an "our baby" were positive for the most part.

> "The twins sort of solidified our blended family," said a mother with a daughter from a previous marriage and two stepsons. "They were everyone's babies and quickly became 'our babies' for the entire family. We found less sibling jealousy than our friends had in their nuclear families. I guess our kids were more used to sharing before the babies were born."

3. Be patient

Stepparents must move slowly, planting the seeds of love and helping them to grow through respect, caring, and appropriate affection. It usually doesn't happen quickly, just as any tender plant grows in its own time.

Patience indeed is a virtue, one that every stepparent must develop. It's often hard, especially when you feel as though you are doing everything you can to befriend your stepchildren and they don't seem to appreciate any of it. The cruel fact is, they may never give you what you want or need in return. Many of the adult stepchildren interviewed said it wasn't until they themselves were grown (and some of them became stepparents), that they fully appreciated the effort made by their stepparent. Some of them even shared that discovery with their stepparent.

Be patient, and even if you don't develop the relationship you would have preferred, take comfort in the knowledge that you have done your very best. Try not to overreact over real or imagined slights. All kids tend to be somewhat thoughtless and even cruel at times. You don't have to be a stepparent to feel unappreciated by your kids.

4. Keep your sense of humor

Almost everyone agreed that a sense of humor is an important ingredient to stir into the blended family pot. Humor softens the rough spots and brings families together. Just remember to never use humor at another person's expense and never permit any of the children to do so either.

5. Learn to compromise

Although finances may prevent you and your new spouse from buying a new home, do so if you can. It's difficult enough for a stepparent to move into an already existing family. When it's the same home as well, the kids (and often the biological parent) may openly or subconsciously resent any changes in decoration, traditions, or actually anything suggested by the stepparent.

6. Respect others

Members of a blended family don't need to agree with each other necessarily, but they must to learn to respect not only the opinions of the other members of their family, but also the privacy and personal possessions of those members. Children often need to share a room with a stepsibling or double up so a stepsibling or half sibling can have their former room. They need to have the confidence that their "stuff" will be safe from prying or curious hands. This is also vital when the parents' other children come to spend time in the blended family home. These tumbleweed youngsters need a private place that's secure for their things as well.

Biological parents should make it clear to their children that they will tolerate no disrespect to the stepparent. The parent also should be careful that he or she is always respectful both in word and action to the stepparent. Children model our behavior.

7. Accept Imperfections

Don't try to be the perfect blended family. If you strive for perfection, you'll only succeed in becoming frustrated. Accept the fact that you and your spouse are not Norman Rockwell models and that *The Brady Bunch* was only a television show, not an actual blended family.

Accept too that there will always be a former spouse, your step-kids' parent, in the picture, even if that person is deceased. Actually, a ghost parent can be more difficult to deal with because his or her faults seem to vanish in the midst, leaving nothing but pictures of perfection. And that's hard to deal with.

8. Be yourself

Be yourself at all times, as kids can easily see through our masks and discern what is really us. You'll wear yourself out trying to play your characterization of the perfect stepparent twenty-four hours a day. Don't try to impersonate what you think the kids (or your spouse) want in a stepparent either. Just be you.

Rather than thinking of yourself as a stepmother or stepfather, consider yourself more as the children's adult friend or a friendly aunt or uncle. It will give you the distance you need while they size you up and is a role you can continue to live with if the kids don't eventually warm up to you. Usually, they'll come around to some degree if they sense you aren't trying to usurp their other parent's role.

9. Give all the family members space

Members of all families need some private time and a place they can go to be alone. It's often more difficult for a blended family because extra space may be in short supply. Instill in all members of the family, even the little ones, respect for a closed door. Create a meditation area outside in the backyard, if possible, with a bench or swing facing a goldfish pond, waterfall, wind chimes, or a flower garden. Stores like Home Depot have many items you can purchase to help you create a relaxing environment for family members to be by themselves for a while.

Arrange seating in your home so there is a cozy spot in the living room or den, behind a screen if necessary, where someone can sit quietly and read a book, write in a diary, or just be alone with his or her thoughts.

Togetherness is wonderful in a fun loving, lively family, but moments of quietude are important too. Try to create room for both in your blended family.

10. Spend time alone with your spouse

Spend time alone with your spouse! Spend time alone with your spouse! It's important enough to say it twice. Your love for your spouse is the reason (hopefully) you became a stepparent. Give your love time, space, respect, and the environment to grow deeper and stronger.

Even if at first your stepkids resent you for marrying their parent, they will see a strong role model for marriage if you make the time to strengthen that marriage. What better gift can you give children than to show that a man and woman can be both friends and lovers and that all marriages don't include fighting, anger, and disloyalty and end in divorce?

When you make time to develop your marital relationship from the beginning, you'll find that you and your spouse are still best friends when the children are grown and move out of your home. If your kids are now still at the age that you need baby-sitters, enlist the grandparents or other members of the extended family to give you that respite. If you and your ES have shared custody, use the time when you don't have the children to play, talk, and be intimate with your new spouse. Leave the housework for later. You can always clean the garage out when the kids are home.

Plan for your future happiness together by starting now to make time for yourselves as a couple.

11. Shed anger and bitterness

Negative emotions can adversely affect both your physical and mental health. What's more, they can become contagious, seeping into the core of your blended family and altering your kids' perceptions of people, marriage, trust, and life in general. It's a heavy load to continue carrying your anger and bitterness from one marriage into another. Drop that burden.

Instead, pick up a positive outlook. You *can* control your thoughts. Whenever a negative thought creeps in, replace it with something positive. Do this until it becomes second nature with you. Many years ago, author Ralph Waldo Emerson wrote, "A man is what he thinks about all day." So rather than ruminating on the bad deal you got from the lawyers during your divorce or the difficulties you still encounter with your ES, focus on the positives in your life—your new wonderful spouse, the great kids in your blended family, your good health, sound mind, and so on. As Norman Vincent Peale preached in his many books, there *is* power in positive thinking.

12. Be honest

Honesty is an important ingredient in any blended family. Many of you have been hurt in the past by a former partner's betrayal of trust. It's a painful wound that takes time to heal. But you can help the healing by insisting on honesty, not just between you and your new spouse, but by the children as well. You can not really begin to trust someone unless you know that what he or she says is true. It clears the air and opens the way to dialogue.

Knowing that you can trust your mate's fidelity gives a sense of security and permanence to your marriage. When you trust your mate, you feel assured that your spouse is honest in business dealings and in money matters with you, his or her ES, and with others.

Discuss the importance of honesty in your family meetings. Show the kids by example that honesty and a sense of trust are important values to you. That means not telling the kids to say you're not home when a solicitor calls. It means returning excess change to clerks when they make mistakes and being honest about the kids' ages when you fly, go to movies, or pay the age-appropriate price at attractions. It means teaching your kids to be truthful, even if it means they may get into trouble when they "fess up." You need to know that you can believe what members of your family circle tell you. Begin now to stress the importance of honesty and you'll be building your blended family on a foundation based on trust.

CONCLUSION

" 'Twixt optimist and pessimist
The difference is droll:
The optimist sees the doughnut,
The pessimist, the hole."

—MCLANDBURGH WILSON
Contemporary author

Are blended families the wave of the future? Will stepfamilies become the norm for our new century? It's hard to tell, but if pressed for an answer, it has to be "probably so." With half of all marriages breaking up and more than half of second, third, and more remarriages being terminated, the trend certainly seems to be going in that direction.

Experts at the Stepfamily Association of America estimate that forty percent of all marriages today include the remarriage of one or both partners. At this writing, one in every six children under eighteen years of age is a stepchild. The children of these marriages and remarriages must quickly learn to be flexible and to interact with a kaleidoscope of relationships and differing parenting styles.

Although this picture may not be Candide's "All is for the best in the best of all possible worlds," it is the world in which we live. And, what's more, many of my interviewees reported that stepfamily living has been a positive experience for them.

> "Becoming part of a blended family has certainly helped my own kids become more tolerant of the idiosyncrasies of others," a midwestern college professor said. "They've learned to compromise with their stepsiblings and to understand that there's more than one way of doing things. We've changed a lot of our 'black-and-white thinking' to rainbows."

Others reported that their kids were flexible, independent, and seemed at ease with themselves in group situations. Another positive that balances some of the negatives involved with the after-effects of divorce and Janus-faced multiple parenting is that youngsters in blended families have a myriad of support systems with (hopefully) many loving grandparents, aunts, uncles, and cousins by the dozens. It's the contemporary version of the village it takes to raise a child.

In practical terms, it also means that with "parenting coalitions," an expression created by stepparenting experts psychologist Emily B. Visher and psychiatrist John S. Visher, there are extra hands for baby-sitting, car pooling, and other child-care duties, more numerous and often deeper pockets for financial emergencies, and more input when vital decisions must be made. In an era where fear of child abuse and kidnapping keeps many parents from hiring strangers in order to take a night out for themselves, this stable of responsible relatives waiting in the wings can become not only a convenience, but also a great comfort.

From the parent's standpoint, blended families also offer a respite from child-care responsibilities from time to time when the youngsters are visiting their other parent. This gives the remarried couple both time and opportunity to rekindle the intimacy of their new relationship without "his" and/or "her" children around—until the "ours" comes along, of course.

As I stated in the beginning of this book, each blended family is unique. What works for you may not be the answer for another couple. It also may take time until you realize that a specific way of doing things does work for you after all. It not only takes time, but it also takes patience, a great deal of patience, along with a sense of humor to develop your co-parenting skills with your ES, as well as with your children's stepparent, your new mate.

In addition, there are so many permeations of what constitutes a blended family—stepparents bringing children to the family, stepparents having no children, parents having noncustodial children by former marriages coming to live on a temporary basis, and so on, that it is impossible to chisel any "musts" in stone.

With all these provisos, the one constant for successful blended families seems to be what Constance R. Ahrons, Ph.D., refers to as being a "pedi-focal family: [one in which] the needs of the children come first." While this in no way suggests that the parents' needs are unimportant, the key to opening the door to a successful blended family must be jointly held by all the adults in the children's world working together to satisfy the kids' needs.

Hopefully, some of the suggestions found in this book concerning communication, consistency, compromise, patience, and discipline, as well as numerous other points will help you become more optimistic as you blend and continue blending your family. As you work out both the anticipated and unexpected lumps that present themselves, remember that they are found not only in step-families, but in all families that are inhabited by humans.

Good luck!

SUGGESTED READING

Ackerman, Marc J., Ph.D., *"Does Wednesday Mean Mom's House or Dad's?"* New York: John Wiley & Sons, Inc., 1997.

Berman, Claire. *Making It As a Stepparent*. New York: First Perennial Library, 1986.

Blau, Melinda. *Ten Keys to Successful Co-Parenting*. New York: A Perigee Book, The Berkley Publishing Group, 1995.

Cocola, Nancy Wasserman. *Six in the Bed: Dealing with Parents, In-Laws and Their Impact on Your Marriage*. New York: A Perigee Book, The Berkley Publishing Group, 1997.

Covey, Stephen R. *The 7 Habits of Highly Effective Families*. New York: Golden Books, 1997.

Doherty, William J., Ph.D. *The Intentional Family*. Reading, Massachusetts: Addison-Wesley Publishing Company, Inc., 1997.

Eckler, James D., *Step-by-Step-Parenting*. Cincinnati, Ohio: Betterway Books, 1993.

Leman, Kevin. *Living in a Step-Family without Getting Stepped On*. Nashville: Thomas Nelson Publishers, 1994.

Lewis, Sheldon, and Lewis, Sheila Kay. *Stress-Proofing Your Child*. New York: Bantam Books, 1996.

Pickhardt, Carl. E., Ph.D. *Keys to Successful Step-Fathering*. Hauppauge, New York: Barron's, 1997.

Visher, Emily B., Ph.D., and Visher, John S., Ph.D. *How to Win As a Stepfamily*. New York: Brunner/Mazel, Inc., 1991.

▪ ADDITIONAL RESOURCES ▪

For more information about stepfamilies, you can write:

· Stepfamily Association of America, 650 J. Street, Suite 205, Lincoln, Nebraska, NE 68508. 1-800-735-0329.

Stepfamily Foundation, 333 West End Avenue, New York, NY 10023. (212) 877-3244.

· Grandparents United for Children's Rights (GUCR), 137 Larkin Street, Madison, WI 53705; (608) 238-8751.

Index